More Chasing God
The Pursuit Continues...

DR. DONALD M. MINTER

Xulon Press
2301 Lucien Way #415
Maitland, FL 32751
407.339.4217
www.xulonpress.com

Printed in the United States of America.

ISBN-13: 978-1-54563-591-9

INTRODUCTION

A Moment On Method:

It is the oldest of the 'spiritual disciplines', an early daily encounter with God's Word, setting the stage for the complexity of life in the day ahead. And this encounter, like all good relationships, ought not be rushed; instead, a time of leisure for two old friends to chat, reflecting on life with all of its twists and nuances. Paul, writing to friends old and new, will be waiting for you each morning. And yes, surprisingly, he has listened carefully to yesterday's conversation and is ready to carry on with previous concerns. So grab a cup of your favorite elixir, settle down, and enjoy your daily conversation. Be warned, his friend, the Holy Spirit, has been known to pop in on occasion to join the conversation. And when He does, no telling what lies ahead. He has been known to be unruly and unpredictable. Just relax and enjoy the dialogue.

A verse-by-verse endeavor is, by definition, cumbersome, yet beneficial to those resisting the temptation to always synchronize the particulars into a neat and tidy whole. Hence, the grand danger of Biblical studies, the ever-present need to organize every verse, every thought, into a well-oiled system, taking care to grind away any rough edges, gnarly particulars ground down for the sake of the whole. Let the rough edges grind on you as they may. Painful at times, but more beneficial than you can imagine.

In the end, only those who learn to 'apply' will return to this daily meeting of the minds. Application, unique and personal, generating a lust for more, a lust that can never be satisfied, is the key to feasting at this daily table. And, fear not, He always provides custom models built with only you in mind.

A final warning for those who choose to journey on. The road could get bumpy, perhaps even impassable at times. Once unleashed, the Serving King rarely provides an autobahn for cruising down life's highway. But keep the peddle to the metal. He is taking you places like you have never dared to imagine. And when you get there, the few, the saints from earlier conversations, will be waiting. And what a glorious time of storytelling will begin…

Chase on, dear friends, chase on…

Don

Day 1

THE SAFETY NET...

"The gospel frees us to confess our sins without fear of condemnation."
—Michael Horton

There is therefore now no condemnation for those who are in Christ Jesus.
(Romans 8:1)

I ntimacy with Jesus inevitably produces an awareness of personal inability regarding rising to levels of *'being and doing'* so easily manifested in the life of the Serving King. And as those chasing after the Serving King draw closer and closer to Him, the details of His *'being and doing'* become readily visible, reminding the chaser of just how very far there is yet to go in becoming like Him. So comes the need for the *safety net.*

The *safety net* provides the much-needed security for those striving to climb the steepest ascents on the trails left behind by the Serving King. Like the trapeze artist recklessly flying through the air comforted by the net below, so those chasing after the Serving King are free to recklessly pursue His way of *'being and doing'*, knowing a free fall to the net is the inevitable result for those daring to risk imitation in the most radical forms. And as the chaser bounces in the *safety net* of failure, so comes the Serving King Himself ready to assist the chaser back onto the trail, back on the steepest terrains, delighted by the effort of those who so gloriously fail, falling into the *safety net* He has prepared. And yes, hesitate not to confess, "I didn't make it," obvious as it seems to be.

You will immediately discover there is no condemnation for those courageous enough to strive to the outer reaches of imitation; only praise for those who recklessly risked all in an effort to mimic the Serving King. Perhaps, more importantly, comes the encouragement to try yet again, to strive beyond today's reach, knowing His Spirit lifts those deepest in the chase to ever new heights, new ways of *'being and doing'*. The Serving King offers only words of encouragement to those brave enough to reach for the fruit on the highest branches. And yes, occasionally, you will indeed reach the highest levels of *'being and doing'*, and oh what a glorious moment, as the Serving King applauds your reckless moment of obedience. Chase on...

Day 2

HORNET WHISPERER...

"Laws are like cobwebs, which may catch small flies, but let wasps and hornets break through." —Jonathan Swift

For the law of the Spirit of life has set you free in Christ Jesus from the law of sin and death...
(Romans 8:2)

Rules and regulations are fine and dandy for the timid, those prewired to submit to the suggestions of others, small flies easily tamed and conquered by the cobwebs of law. But no rule or regulation can tame the raging hornet within the inner being. Resistant to the whims of others, the hornet of the soul refuses to yield, determined to drag even the well-intentioned chaser this way and that, far from the wooing of the Serving King. And so, the hornet seizes the inner being...

But the Law of the Spirit is no mere cobweb easily torn by the torrents of the hornet's fury, rage as it may. No, this is a web of another kind capable of entrapping even the fiercest hornet, taming even the wildest beast, exhausting even the rudest inner being. This is a law of another kind, the Law of the Spirit.

Like the horse whisperers of old, the Law of the Spirit calms the raging hornet, speaking life and liberty into the soul. The hornet, once rebellious toward all law, discovers a new way of *being* and relating to Law, now soothed by the cobwebs of law that once enraged.

And unlike the *law of sin and death*, the *Law of the Spirit* is no mere suggestion of what ought to be in the life of those chasing after the Serving King; instead, it is the *good news* of what will be, the proclamation of what is yet to come. And the *hornet,* once enraged by all suggestion of law, now tamed by the whisperings of the Spirit, soon yearns for obedience. This is a new way of *'being and doing'* for the *hornet* long reigning in the *inner being.* The *Whisperer* speaks often into the life of one set free to chase after the Serving King. And once tamed by the *whispers of the Spirit,* life can never be the same. The *hornet's* fury is forever gone. In its place is a thriving passion toward the Whisperer and His ways. The *Whisperer* has come...

Day 3

IT'S NOT OVER YET...

"It ain't over till it's over!" —Yogi Berra

For God has done what the law, weakened by the flesh, could not do.
By sending His own Son in the likeness of sinful flesh and for sin,
He condemned sin in the flesh...
(Romans 8:3)

Moderns, lovers of immediacy in all of its forms, often struggle with the life-long process of becoming a reflection of the Serving King. And the inability to embrace law in *doing* becomes too great a frustration for some deepest into the quest after the Serving King. Nonetheless, the arrival of *God in the flesh* is a radical proclamation of what is yet possible for those engaged in the war against the flesh. He is the Pathfinder leading all those brave enough to chase along into the final stages of becoming, the implementation of doing. So Paul reminds those deepest into the chase, "...until we all reach unity in the faith and in the knowl-edge of the Son of God and become mature, attaining to the whole measure of the fullness of Christ" (Eph. 4:12).

Some, thinking Jesus free from the imperfections of a flesh like ours, lose heart, ending the chase prematurely, thinking Jesus unfairly equipped, super-charged for the chase toward God-likeness; thus, not really one of us. And indeed, He may be decked out in a body free from the infection of sin, the grand crippler of the human condition. But, perhaps not; perhaps, He really came "...in the like-ness of sinful flesh" ready to condemn sin by victory over it, crushing sin in the flesh, His infected flesh, laying out the path for all who would chase after Him in the power of the Holy Spirit.

And those chasing deepest into the quest after the Serving King discover the necessary missing dimension in completing their quest toward their transforma-tion into the whole measure of the fullness of Christ: *life in the Spirit*. It is only in the power of the Holy Spirit that the potential for *Christlikeness* begins to unfold as Spirit overrides *flesh*, liberating *inner being* to *be and do* just as He did. The *flesh* is much too serious a foe to be condemned and conquered apart from the power of the Holy Spirit. But as serious a foe as *flesh* may be, it cannot resist the persuasive power of the Holy Spirit. It may not be over yet, but the end of the dominion of flesh is just around the corner. Chase on...

Day 4

VALLEY OF THE SHADOW OF DEATH...

"There is no easy walk to freedom anywhere, and many of us will have to pass through the valley of the shadow of death again and again before we reach the mountaintop of our desires." —Nelson Mandela

...in order that the righteous requirement of the law might be fulfilled in us, who walk not according to the flesh but according to the Spirit.
(Romans 8:4)

Flesh is a formidable foe, robust in the battle against the Spirit, determined to fight till the bitter end in a war whose winner was declared long ago. Truth be told, you have walked many miles in the *valley of the shadow of death;* but in days gone by, the *valley of death* felt like home, a comfortable place to dwell, littered with others equally comfortable in the *valley of death.*

Nonetheless, you have heard the whispered challenge to come to the mountaintop, the place where He dwells, a new way of *'being and doing'*. And the path to the top has been clearly marked, highlighted well by Him who came to condemn sin in the flesh, to put it to death, to destroy the works of the devil. The path up is just ahead should you dare to follow His footsteps, condemning sin in your own flesh, putting it to death. So you discover the true meaning of the *valley of death,* the place where sin comes to die its painful death.

It is the place where old ways of *'being and doing'* must die, having been condemned by Him who conquered sin in the flesh. The climb to the mountaintop cannot be sustained by those weighted down with old ways of *'being and doing'*. And yes, their death is often painful, more painful than you could have imagined, old friends dearly missed. And no, they will not die in one comprehensive moment, a mass execution, a brief moment of discomfort. Instead, the *valley of death* must be visited time after time as each familiar way of *doing* dies like those ways ceasing to exist before it.

But death is just the beginning. The journey to the mountaintop is a glorious rediscovering of intended ways of *'being and doing'*, ways full of vigor and life. This is the way of life in the Spirit. You will soon discover life as it was meant to be, a new way of *'being and doing',* His way, life to the fullest. Chase on. There is more life yet ahead...

10

Day 5

MINDSET...

"There are no constraints on the human mind, no walls around the human spirit, no barriers to our progress except those we ourselves erect." —Ronald Reagan

For those who live according to the flesh set their minds on the things of the flesh, but those who live according to the Spirit set their minds on the things of the Spirit.
(Romans 8:5)   Rom, 12:2

L earning to *set the mind* is perhaps one of the last frontiers of Christian Maturity. The early days of the chase after the Serving King are often whimsical, flittering here and there as the S*pirit* leads, a delightful journey into the realms of *grace.* Gone is the *mindset on the flesh.* Equally gone is the *mindset on any particular thing.* Hence, the early days are indeed filled with flittering any which way.

But few are those content to flitter here and there long term in the chase after the Serving King. Instead, the *mind* longs for a place to call home, a place to *set,* a *mindset.* The *flesh,* discontent in its role as a mere distraction, calls for the *mind* to return to its old roosting place, the comforts of home, the old ways of thinking about *'being and doing'.* But the *mind* has gone through a major metamorphosis, no longer able to rest in the old haunts, the old ways of thinking about *'being and doing'.* Instead, it seeks a new *mindset,* a new way of thinking about *'being and doing'.*

And so, the Spirit whispers into the *mind* offering a new place to set up camp, a state-of-the-art roosting spot, a profoundly contemporary way of *thinking,* a brand-new operating system of the highest kind. The invitation to *think this way* is simply that, an invitation to *set the mind* on the things of the Spirit, the Spirit's way of thinking. And every facet of life can be reset, recalculated, refreshed, free to *be and do* in ways the *flesh* knows nothing of. Thus, those chasing after the Serving King must learn to *walk* in the new ways of *thinking.* Fear not the awkward first steps of this novel way of thinking. Like all new ways of *'being and doing', thinking,* too, will come soon enough. Learn to think well and incredible new ways of *doing are* just around the corner as you chase on...

walking in The Light I John 1:7
walk in the spirit Gal 5:16

Day 6

MIND ALTERING...

"It is not enough to have a good mind. The main thing is to use it well."
—René Descartes

For to set the mind on the flesh is death,
but to set the mind on the Spirit is life and peace.
(Romans 8:6)

Thinking well is a critical step toward *altering* the actual circumstances of life, and God is profoundly interested in *altering* life's circumstances. But thinking well is only a first step. Rarely will mere *thinking* bring about the desired life *alterations*. Hence comes the need to *use it well,* to actually *do* what the *altered mind* knows ought to be done. And this, not nearly so easy as it may sound.

A poorly-used mind does little to produce *altered* life; instead, death continues its reign of chaos in the lives of those continuing to *set the mind on the flesh.* Worse yet, once enlightened, a mind filled with opportunities never actualized leaves the *fool,* those who refuse to actualize what the mind knows should be done, in worse condition than before enlightenment. The fool knows things could be radically different, yet continues in all the old ways of *'being and doing'.*

Conversely, a mind *set on the Spirit,* followed by execution, actual *doing,* unleashes *life and peace* toward the doer and all those in proximity. Doers actually unleash *life and peace* upon those fortunates in proximity to the doer. Hence, the *altered* mind has the opportunity to alter reality, the circumstances of life.

The challenge for those chasing after the Serving King is to first *set the mind* on how to chase, and to then actually chase in the manner of the Serving King. In this fashion, the *altered mind* brings about actual change in the circumstances of the many, and the community of faith finds the *life and peace* God offers to His children. And so comes the opportunity to transform the world into the altered reality of the mind.

Day 7

HOSTILITY...

"Those who submit like a child do it because they know that the Father wants only the happiness of His children and that only He knows the way. That is the testimony we must have." —Henry B. Eyring

For the mind that is set on the flesh is hostile to God, for it does not submit to God's law; indeed, it cannot.
(Romans 8:7)

E ven the novice chaser quickly realizes His ways are not our ways, and that is never more evident than when attempting to create a *mindset* by which to set a course for life. More to the point, the renewed *mind* clearly comprehends that a *course change* is called for, mandating comprehensive changes in even the mundane of life. And so, the struggle to change course begins, a battle royal is about to unfold as old ways of *'being and doing'* resist forthcoming change.

The *flesh,* polluted by the infection of sin, is a hostile and formidable foe, even for a mindset on the Law of the Spirit. But the *flesh* has no intention of changing course without a grand and painful struggle. The *flesh* has encountered *wishful thinking* before regarding a grand buffet of ideas from weight-loss, exercise, etc., merely ignoring the *thought of the day,* knowing the mind will return home in the very near future. Tragically, the mind of the chaser does indeed return to the ways of the *flesh* without much delay. Novice chasers are ill-prepared for the necessary battles required for changing course.

So it comes as no surprise as *flesh* is radically empowered by a mind returning to the ways of the *flesh.* And with its old partner back in tow, the *flesh's* hostility toward the ways of God finds expression in a refusal to submit to His ways. The *inner being* languishes as the hostile *flesh* reigns in the day-to-day decisions of life.

But the *Spirit* does not faint in the midst of rebellion, continuing to whisper the wisdom of God's ways into the life of the novice chaser. And the *child,* the novice chaser, soon discovers the truth of the *flesh,* its intent to destroy and maim. Only the *Father* truly delights in the happiness of the child. Therefore, the mind returns to the ways of the *Spirit as it chases on...*

Day 8

FLESH DWELLER...

"The Christian does not think God will love us because we are good, but that God will make us good because He loves us." —C.S. Lewis

Those who are in the flesh cannot please God.
(Romans 8:8)

The desire to *please God* is often late-arriving fruit in the chase after the Serving King. The novice, thinking *pleasing God* a prerequisite to being *loved by God,* rarely comprehends the concept of *pleasing God* as a follow-up to an authentic *loved by God* experience. Hence, intentionality in *pleasing God* is too often polluted by the mistaken intent of earning God's love. And earning God's love simply cannot be done. God's love is a given, a gift, independent of the condition of the one who is loved. And only when it has been received can the possibility of genuinely pleasing God begin to take shape in the present moment.

More importantly, once *loved by God* becomes the foundation of a relationship with God, the desire to *please the one who loves* spontaneously begins to rise up in the one who is loved. It is a fruit of the Spirit. And *pleasing God* is never a matter of *doing,* but rather as simple as *mindset,* or intention of the doer. Hence, it is the *intentionality* of the doing which matters, not the doing itself. Thus, *pleasing God* is a matter of intent, a mindset or disposition of those chasing after the Serving King. All doing will inevitably be less than perfect, but God is pleased.

But the many, having surrendered to the inability to be *good enough* long ago, are often enticed into the *mindset of the flesh,* inadvertently surrendering the opportunity to *please God.* Nonetheless, the Spirit is tenacious in wooing the wayward *flesh dweller* back into the ways of the Spirit, the mindset of the Spirit. And so, the chaser discovers what has been there all along, an ability to *please God* simply by setting the mind on the ways of the Spirit. Thus, the Christian does not think God will be pleased because we are good, but that God will make us pleasing because He loves us. Now the chase on truly begins...

Day 9

IF...

"Advice is like snow—the softer it falls, the longer it dwells upon, and the deeper it sinks into the mind." —Samuel Taylor Coleridge

You, however, are not in the flesh but in the Spirit,
if in fact the Spirit of God dwells in you.
(Romans 8:9)

The *if,* unexpected and yet normative, reflects His way of gently resting upon and within the soul of those chasing after the Serving King. Once present, He rarely causes a ruckus, instead, gently whispering to those anxious to hear. His advice, keys to abundant life, like the falling snow, falls effortlessly into the conscious mind, gently offering wisdom of another kind, His way of *'being and doing'*. But the wisdom of the Spirit, the fruit of His Spirit dwelling deep within, waits patiently to be embraced, prioritized in life, and finally actualized into the realities of day-to-day living, providing specific and powerful instruction for those listening carefully.

But first, it, too, like the fresh snow, must be allowed to sink deep into the conscious and unconscious mind, slowly infiltrating every dimension of life. The warmth of your mind and heart must work its way toward the fresh snow sitting on the surface of the mind. Slowly, the whisperings of the Spirit melt, soaking deeply into the conscious and unconscious mind, penetrating ever deeper into all manner of *'being and doing'*. The soul, nurtured and fed by the fresh falling wisdom of the Spirit, discovers life abundant. The new has come.

But like all things whispered, hearing requires a lack of distraction, focused attention free from disturbances of all kinds. Like fresh fallen snow, divine whispering, wisdom of another kind, is easily crushed and soiled by the footsteps of competing ideas, old ways of *'being and doing'* determined to remain the dominant mode of being. Thus, you will need to carefully protect the fresh fallen snow until it has time to melt, soaking deeply into the soul, refreshing and renewing all that it touches, even transforming the mind. The old has passed and the new has come. Drink deeply all that God provides as spiritual wisdom seeps deep into the *being* of those fortunate recipients of fresh falling snow. Chase on...

Day 10

THE SCULPTOR...

"Culture clash is terrific drama." —Ken Follet

But if Christ is in you, although the body is dead because of sin,
the Spirit is life because of righteousness.
(Romans 8:10)

The Serving King rarely sits quietly in the hidden recesses of the soul; instead, He begins the painstaking process of chipping away the dead and hardened flesh long encrusting the *inner being*. His purpose extends far beyond simply bringing life to the *inner being,* a task relatively easy compared to the infusion of life into the *body* long polluted and rendered dead by the infection of sin. The early stages of the reconstruction usher in the *drama of culture clash* as the ways of the Serving King crash into the long established ways of the *flesh*. And indeed, the ensuing battle is *terrific drama* for all those watching the conflict as the artist chips away. This is indeed a civil war.

The drama unfolds as *Christ in you* begins to unleash His ways of *'being and doing'* into both *inner being* and *body*. The speed of the transformation in the *inner being* occurs quickly as life's motivations transform in the blink of an eye. But the body, long the traveling companion of sin, resists the efforts of the Spirit, determined to *be and do* in the old ways. But *righteousness* is persistent in its efforts to the win the day, even bringing life to that which was dead, even decaying flesh. The sculptor is always at work.

And so, the *Spirit of Life* begins the meticulous process of chipping away the lifeless pieces of the flesh, no longer able to respond to the overtures of the Spirit. Like all great artists giving life to dead pieces of stone, He will work slowly and meticulously, carefully chipping away until the piece of art begins to emerge. And the chase after the Serving King is indeed art at its best. The *drama of what He is creating* will draw the attention of bystanders, each anxious to see what the *Sculptor will create, is creating*. And the drama is just beginning as the chase on intensifies...

Day 11

OPIUM OF THE MASSES...

"Under the pressure of the cares and sorrows of our mortal condition, men have at all times, and in all countries, called in some physical aid to their moral consolations–wine, beer, opium, brandy, or tobacco." —Edmund Burke

If the Spirit of Him who raised Jesus from the dead dwells in you,
He who raised Christ Jesus from the dead will also give life to
your mortal bodies through His Spirit who dwells in you.
(Romans 8:11)

Our common plight, the inability to live out the values we embrace, is known to all persons, none are exempt, each fully aware of the necessity of some *moral consolation* to ease the pain of our universal experience: failure. Karl Marx, frequently credited with the oft-quoted phrase, "It (religion) is the opium of the people," attempted to persuade the masses of the inadequacy of religion, an accurate evaluation of man-made rules and regulations attempting to help others chase successfully after the *Serving King*. But the masses, too discouraged to continue the battle against the *flesh*, turn to the actual *opium of the masses–wine, beer, opium, brandy, tobacco, or most common of all, TV and food*.

But *life in the Spirit* ought never be confused with *religion*. The two have very little in common, other than an intent to move people further along in their efforts to chase after the *Serving King*. Religion can do no more than offer advice on *how to chase after the Serving King*. And for those whose bodies have been *given life*, there is much to be learned from the wisdom of those who have chased along the path previously. Experience has plenty to teach us.

Tragically, *wisdom* is far too often lavished upon those whose *bodies* have yet to receive *life*. And so, the thirsty throng receive countless hours of instruction on how to drink water properly in a land void of water. Little wonder the many turn to life's opiates, moral consolations to those dying of thirst. Living water is the missing *opiate of the people*. Only living water can truly give life.

There is another way, a *living water* (John 4:10), *life in the Spirit,* available to all who thirst after righteousness. This is no mere new way of *doing;* to the contrary, it is the power to *do*, to finally harmonize *doing* with the desires of the heart. Herein is the promise to *"...give life to your mortal bodies"* to all courageous enough to chase on...

Day 12

PURPOSE...

"A man without debts is a man without anything to live for. Debt is collateral for life. It provides you with obligations to others, gives you duty, gives you purpose." —Bauvard

So then, brothers, we are debtors, not to the flesh,
to live according to the flesh.
(Romans 8:12)

The opportunity to experience life comes in the form of an invitation to embrace the potential made available to those intent on chasing after the Serving King. Tragically, the many, long accustomed to an existence separated from life, dragged here and there by the whims of the flesh, never discover the life available to those brought to life by the power of the Spirit. Instead, theirs is an ongoing trek into the old ways of 'being and doing', habits difficult to break, even with the life now flowing through the veins of those born of the Spirit.

But there are those few brothers (and sisters) who seize the day, the opportunity to live in the vitality and life made possible through the indwelling presence of the Holy Spirit. Theirs is a life radically and profoundly different than all previous living. This is a new life, a new way of 'being and doing', empowered by life in the Spirit.

And only those who have truly begun to live can start to comprehend the debt of gratitude to the life-giving Spirit. This is a debt of love, a thrilling opportunity to respond in the ways of the Serving King, to be and do as He does. This obligation is no duty, another burden mandated by law; instead, it's the privilege to finally act out His way of 'being and doing', a radically distinct manner of living only made possible through life in the Spirit. It is the way of finally embracing life to the fullest, the abundant life.

Thus, the arrival of a life with purpose, profound purpose, becoming like Him, begins to show up. But this new trek will require leaving behind the whims of the flesh. Expect the flesh to whine and whimper, begging you to return to the comfortable ways of old. But you have a new obligation, a new way of 'being and doing', a debt to Him who finally has set you free. Chase on in the freedom of your new obligation...

Day 13

SELF-DESTRUCTION...

"Freedom without moral commitment is aimless and promptly self-destructive."
—John W. Gardner

For if you live according to the flesh you will die,
but if by the Spirit you put to death the deeds of the body, you will live.
(Romans 8:13)

The self-destructive behavior of the *flesh* startles even the most optimistic naturalist. The *flesh*, left to its own devices, is quite content to engage in an endless barrage of self-destructive behaviors, appetites of all kind unleashed across the spectrum of human wants and desires. Flesh is indeed its own parasite. Left to its own accord, the *flesh* consumes at will, unconcerned with both short and long-term ramifications. And the so-called *Seven Deadly Sins* are unleashed as the *flesh* consumes at will destroying itself in the process: wrath, greed, sloth, pride, lust, envy, and gluttony.

But the *flesh* need no longer run unconstrained by *moral commitment.* Instead, life in the Spirit is now available to all those relying on the Spirit, *putting to death the deeds of the body,* the seven deadly sins and even its less destructive cousins. Self-destructive behavior of all kinds can now be minimized, even destroyed, as the body surrenders to the *Lordship of the Spirit.*

Nonetheless, the *Spirit* will not do this messy work for you. The *deeds of the body* are under your auspices, your control, your responsibility. Hence, *self-destructive* patterns will not simply disappear as the *Spirit* takes up residence deep in the recesses of your *inner being.* To the contrary, empowered by the Spirit, you must now become the warrior armed and ready to reject the pleas of the body, ready to deal a deathblow to the pathetic whisperings of the flesh as it lay dying at your feet. And you will be tempted to be merciful, to extend *grace* toward the *flesh*, allowing it to co-exist in your chase after the Serving King. But *grace* was never meant to allow the *self-destructive flesh* to continue in the quest after the Serving King. The time for the deathblow has come. Be merciful and end the anguish of the *flesh*, put it to death once and for all as you chase on...

Day 14

LED BY THE LION...

"I am not afraid of an army of lions led by a sheep; I am afraid of an army of sheep led by a lion." —Alexander The Great

For all who are led by the Spirit of God are sons of God.
(Romans 8:14)

I t has changed the course of human history more than any other entity, this army of *sheep* led by the crucified *Lion*. A cursory glance of this army of *sheep* reveals little, if anything, to alarm those upon whom this army descends. They carry no armaments to invoke fear in the hearts of those they approach. And like all sheep, their demeanor instills fear in no one. Still, they march on, changing the course of human history with every step, transforming in ways no army has done before.

Nor do they march in the manner of armies that have gone on before them, perfect unison, order of the highest kind. Instead, each member hears the voice of the *Lion* and marches to His command, unique and descriptive for each sheep. They are unpredictable and self-sacrificing, this army of the crucified *Lion*. Still, for all their diversity, an indescribable unity rises up from their chaotic maneuvering.

Once invaded, no community remains unchanged following the touch of the army of the crucified *Lion*. This army of sheep does not maim and destroy those in their path; instead, they bring life and vitality, enhancing the life of all those fortunate enough to encounter the army of the crucified King, these *sheep*.

Theirs is an obedience of love, a profound desire to follow the crucified King, to be led by Him, used at His discretion. And He views them not as mere soldiers, rather *children of God*, loved and cherished by the King who leads them, the God who called them. These are the *sons of God*, the most powerful force on earth. The gates of hell shall not prevail against this army of sheep, nor shall the kings of the earth. These are the children of the King, the *sons of God*. And so, the army of the crucified King chases on after the Serving King...

Day 15

ADOPTION IN THE PUBLIC SQUARE...

"I liked the idea of the adoption being clear; it was and is not something I am interested in hiding." —Jennifer Gilmore

*For you did not receive the spirit of slavery to fall back into fear,
but you have received the Spirit of adoption as sons,
by whom we cry, "Abba! Father!"
(Romans 8:15)*

Adoption begins with a mere legal declaration, a formal acknowledgment of a change of relationship, often unbeknownst to the adopted. But no legal declaration can transform the heart of the adoptee, even in the Kingdom of God. And the longer the delay in the adoption process, the more difficult the transition to the authentic cry, "Abba! Father!" Neither can the mere proclamation of the *Father* win the heart of the adoptee. Authentic love simply cannot be forced; it is always a two-way street, always must be simply wooed into being.

Early in the quest of those chasing after the Serving King is a hesitation to declare their status as adoptees, newfound children of the King, preferring instead to linger in the shadows of obedience away from the *many* gathering in His name, publicly declaring their adoption into the family of the Serving King. They are often hesitant to declare their new relationship in the public square, fearful of the repercussions of being identified as a *child of the King*, a *sheep* in the army of the *Lion*.

But with time comes familiarity and comfort in the presence of the Serving King, a desire to know Him better. And with a growing knowledge of Him, of how much He loves, so comes the feelings of *phileo*, the love of a family, a willingness to identify first with Him and then with His family, those who call Him *Abba*. The *Church*, the gathering of the *army of sheep*, rises up as those who call Him *Abba* gather to proclaim His name.

Slowly, sometimes painfully slow, comes the desire to make clear the reality of *adoption* in the public square. The heart, now brimming with love for the Serving King, no longer seeks obedience in the safety of the shadows; instead, the *adoptee* boldly declares their status in the family of the Serving King. Secrecy is a thing of the past. Adoption "...was and is not something I am interested in hiding." The *sheep* chase on...

Day 16

THE UNSCIENTIFIC WITNESS...

"If a person is wrong about being right with God, then ultimately it really doesn't matter what he or she is right about?" —Donald Whitney

The Spirit Himself bears witness with our spirit
that we are children of God.
(Romans 8:16)

Moderns love science and its commitment to comment on that which is measurable in a repetitive manner, the scientific method. Fortunately, science remains silent on that which is unmeasurable, refusing to comment on realms beyond its limited reach. Such is the *witness of the Spirit,* this testimony concerning one's adoption into the family of God. But the *witness of the Spirit* is measured by an equally unmeasurable entity, *the human spirit,* able to affirm the *witness of the Spirit.* But moderns, having long ago surrendered all things *spiritual,* often struggle to hear the witness of their own *spirit* as it testifies to the abiding presence of the *Holy Spirit.* Spiritual ears have long gone deaf for a good number of moderns attempting to chase after the Serving King.

But the *Spirit of God* is relentless in its pursuit, its *witness* to the *spirit* of those chasing after the *Serving King.* Still, it is not consistent in its *witness* to each *spirit.* For some, the witness is almost audible, a certainty of mind, clarity resting on an intuitive awareness of the presence of God. For others, a sweeping emotion, a deep and profound emotive awareness of the Spirit's presence. Still others, waves of insight as the Word of God becomes alive, providing insight for day-to-day living.

Regardless of the manner of recognition, the result never varies for those chasing after the Serving King, finally understanding one's status as a *child of God.* The awareness of sonship marks a profound relationship change for those chasing after the Serving King. With inclusion in the family comes the *responsibilities* of being a family member. Gone are the days of merely frolicking in the benefits of hanging out with the family. Like all family members, adoptees are expected to step up and embrace the values of the family. And so, the Spirit testifies, "You are one of us now!" Welcome to the army of sheep, the family of God. Chase on...

Day 17

INHERITANCE...

"I also believe the Bible clearly teaches that there will be those who think they are saved but who are not. They will live out their lives with a false assurance of salvation. They will think of themselves as followers, but a day will come when they'll be pronounced as nothing more than fans." —Kyle Idleman

...and if children, then heirs—heirs of God and fellow heirs with Christ, provided we suffer with Him in order that we may also be glorified with Him.
(Romans 8:17)

I nheritance often fills the mind with visions of unearned fortunes flowing toward those merely at the right place, at the right time, born into the right clan, recipients of undeserved blessing. But Sonship and a consequent inheritance brings unexpected requirements and responsibilities as fully engaged members of the family now called upon to carry on the traditions and ways of the family. And so, the family's way of *'being and doing'* carries on with each new generation. The army of sheep passes His ways onto each new generation.

Thus, the heirs of this *fortune* prepare to embrace His family's way of *'being and doing',* the way of suffering. But moderns are seemingly committed to avoiding suffering at all costs; hence, Paul's call to embrace suffering strikes them as awkward at best. But this inheritance comes with a deposit, a guarantor enabling those fortunate enough to receive the inheritance, to engage in the ways of Him who calls each one into the family of God.

The way of suffering is the fruit, the evidence of His presence, the testimony of the validity of the inheritance. This is no *suffering* in general, the *suffering* of all mankind; no, this is His *suffering,* the fruit of His way of *'being and doing',* the direct by-product of walking as He walked, embracing the path as He leads along the chase. No mere *fan* will embrace His way of *'being and doing'*; no, it is the realm of *sonship* only available to those who have received the inheritance, His way of *'being and doing'.* It is available only to the army of sheep. But rest assured, *suffering* is never the last word; rather, it's merely the gateway to the *glory* that is to come for those daring to chase after the Serving King. Push through and carry on. Chase on into the inheritance that is graciously yours as a member of the army of sheep...

Day 18

DELAYED GRATIFICATION...

"The cross is God taking on flesh and blood and saying, 'Me too.'"
—*Rob Bell*

For I consider that the sufferings of this present time are not worth comparing with the glory that is to be revealed to us.
(Romans 8:18)

M others of a bygone era, one in which children were birthed into this world without the aid of glorious medications relieving volumes of pain, quickly learned to focus on the joy of the child to come rather than the pain and agony of the birthing process. So Paul suggests his decision to focus on the joy to come rather than the *sufferings* of the present moment. But moderns, reared on *"have it your way"* and *instant everything*, rarely respond well to *delayed gratification*, especially regarding the chase after the Serving King. Theirs is a world of quick access and payoffs, even in all things *Spiritual*. And suffering, in all of its hideous forms, deemed unacceptable in the age of *a pill for this and a pill for that*. Delayed gratification is simply too difficult for those reared on "... have it your way."

But most unbearable of all is suffering rising out of faithfulness in the chase after the Serving King. It is unexpected and almost unbearable to those antici- pating a prompt and pleasant reward as they chase faithfully after the Serving King. But faithfulness in chasing after the Serving King often requires a will- ingness to endure unpleasant consequences in the immediacy of the moment. Only those who see the *cross of Jesus* understand the necessity of *suffering* as a stepping-stone to complete identification with the Serving King. It is His way, the fruit of the inheritance made available only to the children of God. Suffering prepares the way for the glory yet to come.

Only those who learn to *consider* the joy that is to come will find the where- withal to endure the *sufferings of the present time*. It is the way of Jesus. And in the same way, the glory of God was revealed in Him, so, too it will be revealed in you. Keep your eyes on the joy that is set before you as you chase on...

Day 19

CARETAKER...

"I maintain that if there is such a thing as a true and honest environmentalist, it's people like Slim and hopefully me, who have been caretakers of the land all our lives, along with the generations before us."
—Wilford Brimley

For the creation waits with eager longing for the revealing of the sons of God.
(Romans 8:19)

The partnership was established in the dawning moments as creation received its caretaker commanded by God to *care for* His glorious garden, "The Lord God took the man and put him in the garden of Eden to work it and keep it" (Genesis 2:15). But sin, a comprehensive agent of corrosion, unleashed its venom on both the caretaker and the glorious creation. Both were languishing in the throws of a fallen condition no longer able to fulfill their divinely-appointed tasks; instead, they engaged in a deadly contest of supremacy. Sadly, a contest neither will win without the redemptive hand of the Creator.

Nonetheless, the creation remains optimistic the caretakers will return to their collective task, abandoning all forms of exploitation toward the creation; instead, coming alongside the creation as a healing agent, allowing the creation to return to its ordained task, providing for the caretaker. No wonder the creation longs for the return of the *sons of God* and the restoring of God's intended balance.

And so, those committed to chasing after the Serving King soon begin to embrace their very first calling, a return to caring for the creation, joining it as a partner likewise yearning to champion the causes of the caretakers. Harmony restored as the *sons of God* embrace HIs creation, and His creation embraces the *sons of God*.

Thus, the comprehensive mission of restoration falls to the *sons of God* as they accept their inheritance, commissioned by God to restore and heal the fractured and broken garden. So the full cycle of God's redemption touches every aspect of the creation. And the creation longs for the revealing, the unveiling, the manifestation of *sons of God* fully engaged in the original commissioning of God. So the Serving King leads God's children into service unto the creation. Chase on as you restore God's creation...

Day 20

DIGGERS...

"Healey's First Law Of Holes: When in one, stop digging." —Denis Healey

For the creation was subjected to futility, not willingly,
but because of Him who subjected it, in hope...
(Romans 8:20)

The current state of affairs, utter chaos on so many fronts in the creation, drives the *many* to dig harder, relentlessly determined to get out of the hole by digging faster. But sooner or later, some wise sage boldly proclaims, "Stop digging!" And so, the few, tired of digging, look for another way out. Exhausted and deeper than ever, the weary finally look up to see the Serving King standing on the edge of life's gargantuan hole, pointing the exhausted diggers to another way out, the path of the Serving King. Here begins the chase after the Serving King. The novice, relieved to be finally heading out of the hole, asks the question, "Why?" It is the question of the ages, "Why God?"

Understand, futility is a powerful tool uniquely suited to garnering the attention of even life's most ferocious diggers, those fervently committed to digging their way out, to finding life apart from the Serving King. Thus, God's subjection of the *creation* to its role in frustrating its caretaker, *in hopes* that the caretakers will ultimately *look up* exhausted from endless digging, ever falling deeper and deeper into the *hole*. The creation points its caretakers to the Serving King.

But *futility* is never the last word; instead, it's only the prod to turn the digger's attention toward the Serving King, toward the way out. And once *futility* has served its purpose, the creation is released from its exercise in *futility*, thrilled to see the arrival of the *sons of God* returning toward their calling to care for God's glorious creation. And hope becomes reality as the fruit of *futility* finally arrives.

Sadly, the courageous efforts of far too many diggers will drive them deeper and deeper into life's hole. Their determination is a deadly motivation as *futility* is held at bay. But the creation always wins in the end. Death and decay the ultimate futility. Alas, *stop digging* and begin the earnest chase after the Serving King...

Day 21

PURPOSEFUL CORRUPTION...

"The corruption of the best things gives rise to the worst." —David Hume

*...that the creation itself will be set free from its
bondage to corruption and obtain the freedom of
the glory of the children of God.
(Romans 8:21)*

Corruption, painful and lasting as it may be for the creation, like futility, is never the last word. Nonetheless, in the meantime, the *worst* rising out the corruption is often long-lasting and painful for those caught in the resulting chaos. The *worst* serves as a reminder to all on the journey of life of the brokenness invading the day-to-day experiences of the living, and the hope for healing and redemption available to those wise enough to seek after the Serving King.

Thus, *freedom* has equally arrived into the lives of those chasing after the Serving King, and with *freedom* comes hope for deliverance for both the children of God and the creation. But *freedom* is not absolute nor complete for the children of God nor the creation; instead, it's relative and powerful to the degree to which it has been unleashed on the human condition. Still, there is much that can be done as the children of God turn their attention to the brokenness of the creation.

The creation waits patiently for the children of God to embrace their new-found freedom in hopes the children of God will engage in the healing of the creation, long wounded and crippled by the excesses of those consigned to care for the creation. And as the wounds inflicted by the intended caretakers are healed, so the creation regains its ability to provide for the caretakers, just as the Creator intended. The partnership restored.

But the caretakers can do no more than clean up the mess they have created. There is more to be done, but only by the hand of Him who subjected the creation to its futility. And His hand will only move toward full restoration when the purpose of corruption has been completed, until all missing chasers have arrived. Chase on until every lost one has been found...

Day 22

INCOMPETENT...

"Right now, we don't have a very good relation with creation." —Pope Francis

For we know that the whole creation has been groaning
together in the pains of childbirth until now.
(Romans 8:22)

The naturalist, optimistic and confident regarding the intentionality of the creation, operates under the illusion of a benevolent *creation,* kind and well organized, competent in bringing about *well-being* for all of the creation, including humanity. But no such harmony actually exists in the world as we know it. Instead, the *creation groans in the pains of childbirth,* contorting this way and that in the attempt to give birth to a harmonious existence for every dimension of the creation.

But every dimension of the creation has been tainted in some way by the infection of sin, and the subjection to futility distorting the competency of the creation in totem. Hence, every aspect of the creation is, to one degree or another, off-kilter, rendering the creation incompetent in its efforts to fulfill its initial responsibility. The incompetent creation grinds along inflicting pain and chaos in its well-intentioned efforts to function harmoniously.

Further, the *off-kilteredness* of the creation lacks consistency, creating an unpredictability for those seeking to gain a peaceful harmony with a broken creation, rendering the creation a dangerous partner. And so, all of the creation groans in its incompetence, longing for the reconciliation that only God can offer, a reconciliation yet to come. But the effort has been initiated and the process is proceeding, gaining ground with every passing day. The caretakers have finally risen from their slumber.

The caretakers, incompetent themselves, struggle in their efforts to walk harmoniously with an unpredictable creation. Still, the birthing process has begun, and the restoration of the relationship between caretaker and the creation is underway. The day is drawing nearer when caretaker and creation will return to their intended partnership. The pains of childbirth have begun, and the arrival of the Kingdom of God has begun. Chase on until completions arrive...

Day 23

FINAL FRONTIER...

"Your current circumstances are part of your redemption story He is writing."
—Evinda Lepins

*And not only the creation, but we ourselves, who have the first fruits of the
Spirit, groan inwardly as we wait eagerly for adoption as sons,
the redemption of our bodies.*
(Romans 8:23)

I t is the grand frustration of the chase after the Serving King, the concluding chapter, the last vestige of corruption, the final frontier of adoption as children of God: *the redemption of our bodies.* The body, horribly infected, stuck in decay, destined for degeneration, sees little, if any, of the redemption that is to come. So the child of the King moans in the frustration of ongoing disrepair, longing for the redemption the *inner being* knows already. But the redemption of the *inner being* will not extend to the *body,* not in this life. A momentary healing, perhaps, but nothing more. And so, those chasing after the Serving King learn to do so within the limitations of ongoing decay.

But once the *inner being* finds redemption, a profound and increasingly comprehensive transformation of *being*, it longs to come to the aid of the *flesh,* the *body,* assisting it in finding health and restoration. But the inner being can do no more than bring temporary relief to a body doomed to decay. Still, the reclamation of the doomed *flesh* is one of the grand dimensions of those deep into the chase.

Thus, one of the grandest miracles of all begins to unfold in the lives of those chasing deep into the quest after the Serving King. The *body,* decrepit and decaying as it may be, is claimed by the redeemed *inner being* and refocused to the grand calling of the Serving King. It, too, weakened and staggering as it may be, begins to embrace the ways of the Serving King. Even the boorish dimensions of *flesh* are touched, restoring life-giving patterns of *'being and doing',* renovating even the mundane of eating, sexuality, exercise, etc.

The *body,* once falling headlong into patterns of destructive and foolish behavior, now finds relief in the healthy ways of *'being and doing'* made possible by the *first fruits* of life in the Spirit. Chase on into the health that awaits...

Day 24

FINITE REALITIES...

"We must accept finite disappointment, but never lose infinite hope."
—Martin Luther King

For in this hope we were saved. Now hope that is seen is not hope.
For who hopes for what he sees?
(Romans 8:24)

This *hope* is no mere wishful thinking; rather, it's a first fruit of redemption peeking over the realms of decay as the *inner being,* already redeemed and transformed, raises its head and testifies to the transformation of the *body* that is yet to come. The *inner being* knows the *saved* which has occurred in the present moment, releasing the *inner being* from the decay of self-absorption, the slavery to sin, the old ways of *'being and doing'*. So, the inner being proclaims the goodness of life to come, even for the body of death.

But the redemption to come is an *almost but not yet* affair. It is a work for another time and another place, yet guaranteed by the *already* that has arrived in the *inner being.* So the *inner being* no longer hopes for redemption; instead, it knows redemption, here and now. And it is the testimony of the *inner being* which speaks life into the body, providing hope for its redemption in the here and now.

The *good news* for the body is the power of the *Spirit* to breathe life and vitality back into decaying flesh, enabling long-entrenched patterns of foolish behavior to be reversed. The body, once a playland for sin, now partners with the *Spirit* to enact righteousness, God's way of *'being and doing'* in the present moment. Redemption has arrived.

Nonetheless, there will always be *finite disappointment* for those chasing after the Serving King; and not because of a lack of progress. Instead, there is a profound desire to mirror the transformation of the *inner being*. But, alas, the *finite disappointment* points to the transformation of intent now driving the child of the King to be *all* that the *inner being* calls it to be. And there is a day coming when the redeemed body will no longer hope. For hope will have become reality for all those who have chased faithfully after the Serving King...

Day 25

PATIENCE IN THE UNSEEN...

"Patience is bitter, but its fruit is sweet." —Jean Jacques Rousseau

But if we hope for what we do not see, we wait for it with patience.
(Romans 8:25)

B ecoming is a lifelong process, extensive and complicated, full of ups and downs, a three steps forward, two steps backward kind of affair. Hence, *patience* is a necessary entity for those determined to continue deep into the trek after the Serving King. But *patience* is only necessary for those with heightened expectations, a determination to become what God has called those chasing after the Serving King to be.

The *many*, ill-suited for *patience*, too often abandon the quest, discouraged by the seeming lack of progress. *Patience* for the *many* is nothing more than a lack of effort, a contentment with the status quo, a mere waiting for God to bring about radical change in those who do nothing. Such *patience*, modeled by the many, produces little, if anything, in those chasing after the Serving King. They have simply decided to sit down and wait for the Serving King to initiate any and every dimension of *becoming.* Theirs is a *patience* rooted in impotence.

But there is another kind of *patience*, a fruit of the Spirit, a willingness to engage in His ways of *'being and doing'*, understanding the fruit of such effort will appear only in days that are yet to come. Life apart from His ways of *'being and doing'* has established deeply entrenched patterns and habits that can only be rooted out one step at a time. Implementing new ways of *'being and doing'* unlocks the pathway to that which is yet to arrive, one step at a time.

Still, the *unseen* is coming, often visible to others long before the mirror reveals the *unseen* in the eyes before the mirror. Look closer. The *unseen* is emerging slowly but surely in the life of the one chasing deeply into the quest after the Serving King. Indeed, "Patience is bitter, its fruit is sweet!" Chase on, the sweetest fruit is just around the bend...

Day 26

HE UNDERSTANDS YOU...

"Fear not because your prayer is stammering, your words feeble, and your language poor. Jesus can understand you." —J. C. Ryle

Likewise the Spirit helps us in our weakness. For we do not know what to pray for as we ought, but the Spirit Himself intercedes for us with groanings too deep for words.
(Romans 8:26)

The novice, brimming with confidence and the certainty of the beginning steps, knows little of the *weakness* that is yet to come, but come it will. *Weakness* only stalks those most committed to the deeper regions of the quest after the Serving King; hence, *weakness* appears in those deep into the trek after the Serving King. The less than radically committed, feeling the first twinges of fatigue, simply sit down and rest, pausing long enough to catch their breath before returning to the less strenuous sections of the trail. But the committed, understanding *weakness* to be a part of the experience, soon rise again, continuing on with *weakness* as a constant traveling companion.

Weakness exploits two critical aspects of the human experience. First is the staggering *ignorance* of His ways of *'being and doing'*. His ways are simply not your ways. Unfamiliar with the Serving King's ways, the novice stumbles around blindly seeking to discover His ways of *'being and doing'*. But more problematic is the simple *fatigue* that often accompanies those who discover His ways of *'being and doing'* and chose to engage.

The discovery of His ways of *'being and doing'* is the by-product of the Spirit's intercession on your behalf. His task is to lead you into *truth*, in the King's ways of *'being and doing'*, and to empower you toward obedience in the midst of *weakness and fatigue*. But you will have to learn to live with *weakness*; it is the by-product of those chasing deepest into the trail of the Serving King and the means by which the trekker is forced to *lean on the everlasting arms*.

And rest assured, in the midst of your staggering and mumbling, "Jesus understands you" and takes great delight in coming to your aid. And yes, the fatigue will pass, but only for the moment; there are still yet higher mountains to climb and lots of fatigue yet ahead. Chase on...

Day 27

THE PRATTLE TRANSLATOR...

"Intercession is putting yourself in God's place; it is having His mind and His perspective." —Oswald Chambers

And He who searches hearts knows what is the mind of the Spirit, because the Spirit intercedes for the saints according to the will of God.
(Romans 8:27)

Most intercession, lacking intimate knowledge of God's ways of *'being and doing'*, becomes mere babbling in the presence of God, *prattling* from well-intentioned advisors, ignorant of God's perspective. Fortunately, the Serving King has provided a translator, an intercessor, who knows *the mind of God*, able to approach God with life's concerns framed in a point of view in line with the *perspective of the King.* Thus, all intercession must be transliterated by the *prattle translator.* And so, the *Spirit intercedes for the saints* in all matters pertaining to the Kingdom of God. It is what He does.

Acquiring the *mind of* God is a complicated and fragile process. But deep into the trek after the Serving King, an amazing development begins to occur. The *prattle,* well-intentioned as it may be and, perhaps, even entertaining to the Serving King, begins to transform, evolving into the *perspective* of God, the concerns of God, even the very mind of God. Suddenly arrives that glorious moment in which the *prattle translator* simply smiles knowing the child of the Serving King has finally learned to speak the language of the Serving King. Such is the fruit of a *renewed mind,* those learning to *be and do* in the manner of the Serving King, finally able to communicate directly with Him.

But fear not should the *prattling* return. The *prattle translator* stands by ever ready should the need arise for translation to the King. He is relentless in searching the heart and translating to the King the secrets of the heart. And most importantly of all, the *prattle translator* is committed to making the language of God available to those listening carefully to the dialogue between Spirit and the Serving King. Listen carefully and stand in awe, as you begin to comprehend the ways of the Serving King. There is much more to hear as you chase on...

Day 28

MACRO OR MICRO?

"...know that everything in life has purpose. There are no mistakes, no coincidences, all events are blessings given to us to learn from."
—Elisabeth Kubler-Ross

And we know that for those who love God all things work together for good, for those who are called according to His purpose.
(Romans 8:28)

The novice often begins the trek after the Serving King fully persuaded life is nothing more than random occurrences each unconnected to the others, inflicting consequences upon those they haphazardly run into. They use the language of *luck* or *unlucky* to describe the effects on those randomly impacted by the arbitrary occurrences in life. Such is the culture of functional deism in the modern landscape; the grand clockmaker disengaged, letting the clock simply run its course.

But sooner or later, as the complexity of life becomes clear, the randomness begins to disappear into complicated patterns of life beginning to take shape. The novice trekker soon recognizes purpose and intentionality in the complex patterns taking shape. But the novice trekker sees only the *macro*, broad sweeping intentionality disconnected from the randomness unfolding in the minor details. But it is in the details of life that the hand of God is most easily recognized.

Indeed, deeper into the quest comes the awareness of *intentionality,* purpose in the details, the minor dimensions of life, a seamless connectivity in the *micro* of life. Gone is the illusion of *randomness* and in its place the sudden awareness of purpose in the details, the micro of life. And with the awareness of purpose in the details comes the ability to endure the uncomfortable and painful in life. It is *purpose* that makes the awful doable, endurable, meaningful. God in the details makes life doable.

The grandest gift of all is the ability to see the *purpose of God* in the midst of the seeming random chaos. Sadly, few seem to see His invisible hand. But those who do, even for just a moment, discover *purpose.* Now having seen the hand of God, fully persuaded God is at work also in the minutia of the ugly, comfort is offered even to the 'unlucky'. *Purpose* is the key to seeing *all things work together for good.* Chase on until you finally see His invisible hand...

Prone to wander

Day 29

CALLING...

"The one aim of the call of God is the satisfaction of God, not a call to do something for Him." —Oswald Chambers

And those whom He predestined He also called, and those whom He called He also justified, and those whom He justified He also glorified.

Rom. 8:29 (Romans 8:30)

The move toward *the image of His Son* is the by-product of being *called*, a persuasive manifestation of the presence of God, drawing the hearer toward a way of *'being and doing'* reflective of the *'being and doing'* of the Son. The *call* initiates the *image* of *the Son* as it takes shape in the life of those chasing after the Serving King, persuading and shaping the chaser, gently and consistently, as the quest after the Serving King moves deeper and deeper into *being* of the Son.

The point of this incredible transformation, reflecting the *image of the Son*, is not to prepare the trekker for this or that form of service, but simply to satisfy God who calls. The novice, thinking *doing* the key to satisfying the King, slowly discovers the more essential dimension of *being*. And so, the *call* causes the trekker *pause* as *doing* often prevents the necessity of *being*. It is in the solitude of the *pause* that the *being* of the Son takes shape in the encounter with Him. So the trekker discovers the requisite of *pause*, the foundation of all that is to follow.

And the trekker, deep into the quest after the Serving King, discovers a new and profound motivation in life, ushering in meaning and purpose to all of life's *'being and doing'*, an unembellished desire to simply *satisfy* the God who calls. Hence, life becomes meaningful for the trekker, not because of the glorious successes of *'being and doing'* as the Son even when reflecting His image; rather, it is by the straightforward satisfied smile of the Father. Soon, the smile of the Father becomes the driving force of life, the purpose in all of life's *'being and doing'*. And those who discover His smile find the only motivation ever needed for life. Seeing God smile empowers all those desiring to chase on...

Day 30

WORK IN PROGRESS...

"We all want progress, but if you're on the wrong road, progress means doing an about-turn and walking back to the right road; in that case, the man who turns back soonest is the most progressive." —C. S. Lewis

What then shall we say to these things? If God is for us,
who can be against us?
(Romans 8:31)

T he chase after the Serving King is laden with *against us,* those unpleasantries often littering the path of the Serving King. And the novice, filled with expectations of pleasantries associated with a life aligned with the Serving King, often pauses to consider the possibility God is displeased, given the unpleasantries experienced in the present moment. Further, the illusion God is displeased is readily associated with the unpleasant reality of the many aspects of your *'being and doing'* still not reflecting the image of the Son. After all, the novice chaser is still a *work in progress,* far removed from what shall be in the days yet ahead.

But God has never been pleased or displeased by your particular *doing;* rather, by the simple reality you are either *in Him or not.* God's pleasure with you has no bearing on you at all. His pleasure is solely connected on seeing you in Him and Him in you. The Serving King is the source of all pleasure that God finds in you. He is the pleasure of God.

Still, there are many consequences to the life that have been lived, are being lived, and shall be lived in the days to come. And those consequences are the mere by-products of actions taken, and, as such, give no direct indication of God's pleasure or displeasure. He will continue to see you in Him and only in Him. He sees Christ in you. Only the righteousness of the Serving King has any bearing on the Father's pleasure toward you, and only as the Serving King makes His righteousness available toward those engaged in the chase after Him.

Only the novice lives in the illusion of personal righteousness worthy of pleasing the King. But this too shall pass. Soon, like all those who have gone before, the novice comes to understand only the Son can please the Father. Chase on in the fullness of the Son...

Day 31

VALUED...

"You can grow up with literally nothing and you don't suffer if you know you're loved and valued." —Esperanza Spalding

He who did not spare His own Son but gave Him up for us all,
how will He not also with Him graciously give us all things?
(Romans 8:32)

The temptation to rescue the Son must have been incredibly difficult to endure, even for God; nonetheless, no such rescue comes for the Son. Instead, the Father resists rescuing the Son even as the Son agonizes in His proclamation of abandonment, "My God, My God, why have You forsaken Me?" (Matthew 27:46). The motivation for Father and Son is the redemption of creation, specifically, those who chase after the Crucified King. So, the Father withdraws from the agony of the Son, and the sensation of abandonment comes crashing down upon the Son.

But more problematic must have been the temptation to crawl down from the cross, to abandon the calling of the Father, to release the rebellious creatures to their well-deserved demise, to simply walk away from paying a bill that was not His own; nonetheless, the Serving King remained on His painful perch. In obedience to the Father's intention to not *spare His own Son,* and His love for those who would respond to His offer of redemption, the Son remains on the cross, faithful to His appointed moment.

And so comes the discovery of how little is needed in life for those who know they are loved by Him who gave so much. The Father's lavish sacrifice reminds all chasing after the Crucified King of how little is needed in life when you know *you're loved and valued.* What else could be given for those who have received so much? What else could be desired by those who have received the renewal of the *inner being,* the literal transformation of *being* itself? Thus, the children of God chasing after the Serving King discover life's grandest secret, *so little is needed by those who know they are loved and valued.* How easy the trek for those ladened with so little in the chase after the Serving King. Your load is light, chase on...

Day 32

EXPECTATIONS...

"Expectation is the mother of all frustration." —Antonio Banderas

Who shall bring any charge against God's elect? It is God who justifies.
(Romans 8:33)

L abels create expectations, *the mother of all* frustration, and none more than Christian, Thus, charges are quick to come from those whose *expectations* are not met. And yes, many are those who will create standards to be measured against, both inside and outside of the community of faith. And no, you will not meet the standards they have created for you, nor will anyone else who is deter-mined to chase after the Serving King.

Still, the novice chaser, fearful of judgment by others, is often quick to sur-render to the expectations of those unfamiliar with the *calling* of God, His way of *'being and doing'*. And so begins the flurry of activity all for the sake of meeting standards that mean nothing to God, standards sanctified by sincere and well-in-tentioned people, but worthless before God nonetheless. Therefore, the novice must surrender the temptation to be measured by others.

For those in Christ Jesus there can be no *charges, having* surrendered all claims to self-justification before God. There is no pretense of self-righteousness before God. Further, they have resisted the temptation to allow others to mea-sure them as well. Hence, there is no charade of *making the grade* or earning one's standing before the King, simply because there is no grade to be made.

The Crucified King is the only standard that matters, and He has fulfilled that standard, offering His righteousness to all those who would chase after Him. Thus, one's relationship to the Serving King is the only standard of any value to the *God who justifies*. And those who are found *in Him* shall be justified by the declaration of God, *not by works, lest any man should boast.* Therefore, you are free to recklessly chase after the Serving King, freed from the fear of judgment, liberated to simply *be and do* as the Serving King leads...

Day 33

THE INTERNAL JUDGE...

""The condemnation is not that I am born with a heredity of sin, but if when I realize Jesus Christ came to deliver me from it, I refuse to let Him do so..."
—Oswald Chambers

Who is to condemn? Christ Jesus is the one who died—more than that, who was raised—who is at the right hand of God, who indeed is interceding for us.
(Romans 8:34)

The surrender of *self-righteousness* is a dramatic moment in the life of the those chasing after the Serving King. Stripped of all illusions of *good,* the trekker recognizes the need for an intercessor, one who will stand before the King and plead the case of those stripped of all pretense. And so, Jesus rises from His seat and comes to the aid of all those who have surrendered self-justification in all of its subtle forms. He is *the Intercessor,* the only One.

But expectation often creeps back into the life of those who begin to *'be and do'* in the manner of the Serving King. With competence in His ways of *'being and doing'* comes the return of self-justification, the temptation to assist Jesus in providing righteousness for the Father to see. And with every instance of self-justification comes the return of the internal judge, personal condemnation for each and every failure to measure up to personal standards thought attainable by one so deep in the chase after the Serving King. Success in *'being and doing'* often breeds expectations and consequent condemnation. Resist the temptation.

And yes, even the attempt to self-justify, and the consequent folly of personal condemnation, falls under the grace of Him who intercedes for those trying so hard to be worthy of the calling of the Serving King. Fortunately, for all those chasing after the Serving King, the Intercessor will not allow any In Him to represent themselves before the Father. He is the Intercessor in all moments. Nor will He allow any self-condemnation. There is no condemnation for those who are in Christ Jesus. He has set you free from all who would bring charges against God's elect, including yourself. There is no one who can condemn those who are in Christ Jesus. Chase on in Him...

Day 34

DANGEROUS PLACES...

"The surf that distresses the ordinary swimmer produces in the surf-rider the super joy of going clean through it. Apply that to our own circumstances, these very things—tribulation, distress, persecution, produce in us the super joy; they are not things to fight." —Oswald Chambers

Who shall separate us from the love of Christ? Shall tribulation, or distress, or persecution, or famine, or nakedness, or danger, or sword?
(Romans 8:35)

The Serving King often treks in dangerous places, places filled with tribulation, famine, nakedness, danger, and swords. In fact, He does His best work in *dangerous places, rescuing the wounded;* and those who chase along after Him soon discover they too are faced with the same environment when in close company with the Serving King. It is the expected fruit for any who take Him serious in His "Pick up your cross and follow Me." All walk the same trail.

The novice, unfamiliar with the trails tread by Jesus, often mistakes the terrain of His meanderings for a lack of love by God toward those chasing after His Son; when, in fact, the consequences of being on the trails He walks are the very circumstances giving rise to fears and doubts. The novice, fearful of what may yet come, often seeks to persuade Jesus to leave *dangerous places,* to reside in sanctuaries safe from the turmoil of a broken land. Nonetheless, pleading with Him will do no good. He cannot be dissuaded from *'being and doing'* in the places that need Him most. He is a man of danger. So are those who chase after Him.

Thus, it is in the *dangerous places* that Jesus most often encounters those who need Him most. So He leads HIs followers into those places avoided by so many of the religious and self-protecting. It is those who trek after the Serving King who encounter the *dangerous places* of this world. He rarely goes alone. You too must go with Him.

And yes, there will be moments of fear in the *dangerous places* of this world. Fear of the danger itself, and, sometimes, fear that God has abandoned you in this place, leaving you alone in the *dangerous place.* But you are never alone in the dangerous place. The Serving King is with you, and you have entered a very special place where only those chasing deepest after the Serving King find the love that rises above mere circumstance. Chase on into the dangerous places...

Day 35

MIDDLE OF THE ROAD...

"Standing in the middle of the road is very dangerous; you get knocked down by the traffic from both sides." —Margaret Thatcher

As it is written, "For your sake we are being killed all the day long; we are regarded as sheep to be slaughtered."
(Romans 8:36)

Few are those who follow the Serving King into the most *dangerous places,* where neither the Serving King nor His followers are well received by the commoners unfamiliar with the desires of God. Paul's use of Psalm 44:22 points to a time when the people of God were slaughtered like sheep as an offering to gods by those knowing nothing of what God truly desires. So those who killed the Serving King believed they were honoring God by the death of His Son.

But those who chase after the Serving King, knowing the dangers awaiting followers of the King, merely join the throng of those who have embraced *all these things* before them. Theirs is a *slaughtering* of the highest kind, an embracing of the call of the King, a destiny prepared for the *grand champions* of those chasing deepest after the Serving King.

But there is another place where many are crushed, slaughtered as sheep, run over by the multitudes racing here and there. It is the *middle of the road*, a gathering of the undecided and fearful, a place of pause for those who embarked on the chase after the Serving King only to see the *all these things* ahead. These are the poor souls too fearful to finish crossing the road. Tragically, so afraid to finish the trek to the other side, these *middle of the roaders* are likewise crushed by the *traffic from both sides.*

However, there are no grand champions for those slaughtered in the middle of the road. Their deaths are a *greek tragedy.* Enlightened souls unable to embrace the glorious fate waiting for those who faithfully embrace the *all these things.* Only in the *middle of the road* do they discover the fate waiting for all persons: death. Better to die the death of *slaughtered sheep* than to become *road kill* in the *middle of the road.* Chase on to the other side of the road...

Day 36

THE GRADUATION…

*"It is dangerous to exist in the world. To exist is to be threatened.
We must live with threats." —Adam Levin*

*No, in all these things we are more than conquerors through Him who loved us.
(Romans 8:37)*

Moderns, like all those who have preceded them, fear death greatly. Death is the ultimate opponent, a foe stalking each and every soul walking the earth, finally, momentarily, victorious over all who live. Thus, to live is a very dangerous proposition, and great energy is spent attempting to avoid the unavoidable, delaying the inevitable as long as possible.

But life is a classroom, a very dangerous classroom, preparing those chasing after the Serving King for the journey that is to come once school is over. Hence, death is not an ending, but, rather, a *graduation*, unleashing the graduate to the life that is to unfold. The novice, unaware of the pending *graduation,* fearful of embracing the threats, often misses the lessons needed to be learned to prepare the victor to be more than just a champion, but, instead, a *grand champion,* one who has experienced and learned from all of the lessons life has to teach.

But those who trek deep into the dangerous quest after the serving King, who experience *all these things* before dying in Christ Jesus, soon discover they are conquerors of the highest order, grand champions ready to engage in the victorious life awaiting each and every *grand champion.* However, understand the *all these things* are often avoidable, side stepped with ease, missed entirely by those too fearful to follow the Serving King into *all these things.*

Resist the temptation to avoid *all these things,* so that upon the day of your graduation from the school of life, you, too, having been prepared and learned the lessons, will be a *grand champion* of the highest order. Chase on, there are still many lessons ahead for those daring to be *grand champions…*

Day 37

ASSURANCE...

"The world is indeed full of peril, and in it there are many dark places; but still there is much that is fair, and though in all lands love is now mingled with grief, it grows perhaps the greater." — J.R. Tolkien

For I am sure that neither death nor life, nor angels nor rulers, nor things present nor things to come, nor powers, nor height nor depth, nor anything else in all creation, will be able to separate us from the love of God in Christ Jesus our Lord.
(Romans 8:38-39)

Those who have been loved, and have loved in return, know the agony of love eroded, washed away in tomorrow's arrival. And those who determine love only by life's ever-changing circumstances are always vulnerable to the erosion of love when love's circumstances change, and change they will. Change of circumstance is an ever-present reality for those chasing after the Serving King. He is always on the move toward those who need Him most and, thus, the ever-changing circumstances of life. Nothing stays the same, not even in the chase after the Serving King.

But there is another kind of love, fiercely independent of circumstance, radically dependent upon relationship. This love knows no erosion when the trek after the Serving King ushers in new circumstances, some fraught *full of peril*. The circumstances giving birth to His *love* are permanently etched in the pages of history, the Crucified King, giving His life for the sake of the world He has come to save, "For God did not send His Son into the world to condemn the world, but in order that the world might be saved through Him" (John 3:17).

The *circumstance of the cross* never changes; instead, it is a constant reminder of love manifested on the cross for the world He came to save. The cross serves to remind all who would doubt in the circumstances of tomorrow, to reflect, to see the ever-present foundation of the love that can never change. And this love extends universally to *the world*, to every facet of the creation, every person willing to join the *whosoever will*.

And when in doubt, simply look back to the cross, the eternal proclamation of God's love for His creation. Nothing can separate us from the love of God in Christ Jesus our Lord. The cross is a permanent testimony to His undying love. Chase on...

Day 38

THE AGONY OF SALVATION...

"Behind every trial and sorrow that He makes us shoulder, God has a reason."
—*Khaled Hosseini*

*I am speaking the truth in Christ—I am not lying; my conscience bears me
witness in the Holy Spirit—that I have great sorrow
and unceasing anguish in my heart.*
(Romans 9:1-2)

S alvation is never meant to be an isolated affair, a party of one, a grand celebration in the privacy of one's own home, nor even a dinner party for two as
you and Jesus celebrate your narrow escape. Instead, *salvation* is always meant
to be a communal event, a big block party in which dear family and friends gather
to celebrate the glory of the Kingdom of God finally arriving in the lives of those
who have found salvation. It is the grandest of all communal experiences.

But those who love others deeply suffer the anguish of the absence of those
dearest in life at the glorious celebration that is new life in Christ. And many are
those whose party is missing the presence of those most loved and cherished
in life. So the Apostle Paul acknowledges the *unceasing anguish in my heart,*
robbing him of joy, ushering in the dark side of salvation, the *agony of salvation,*
the nagging remorse over those still not in attendance at the grand banquet of
the Serving King.

But this is an agony of a special kind, a motivating force in the life of those
touched by the grace of salvation, thrusting the revelers back into the world of
those still untouched by the trek of the Serving King. It is the constant reminder
that the time for partying has not yet come. There will be plenty of time for
grandiose celebrations in the days yet ahead. But today is not that day. Today
is the day to join the trek of the Serving King as He continues His search for all
those still neglecting their invitation to the grand wedding feast. "Just so, I tell
you, there will be more joy in heaven over one sinner who repents than over
ninety-nine righteous persons who need no repentance" (Luke 15:7). Time to
continue the chase, the party is yet to come...

Day 39

THE MADNESS...

"When love is not madness it is not love." —Pedro Calderón de la Barca

For I could wish that I myself were accursed and cut off from Christ for the sake of my brothers, my kinsmen according to the flesh.
(Romans 9:3)

Those who love deeply know the horrible anguish of partying at the grand banquet while loved ones languish in the lonely streets of sin. And those who love deepest know an unbearable agony, a *madness* consuming the soul, driving the burdened soul toward lavish extravaganzas, even the fulfillment of the Serving King's instruction, "Greater love has no one than this, that someone lay down his life for his friends" (John 15:13). Such is the madness of those who love deepest, in the way of the Serving King, in the way of self-sacrifice mimicking the way of the Serving King's cross. And many are those who speak the language of *love*, but few are those actually willing to lay down life for the sake of those loved ones still outside the community of the Serving King.

Still, there is a *madness* known to an incredible few, those willing to surrender life itself, *cut off from Christ*, for the sake of those still wandering in the insanity of sin. And this *madness* cannot be generated even by the best intentions of those chasing after the Serving King. No, this *madness* is the by-product of the indwelling Spirit of the Serving King driving those seized by such *madness* to extreme levels of self-sacrifice out of devotion to the Serving King and those He loves.

But the Serving King will allow no such exchanges by those chasing deepest after Him. No man can buy salvation for another, try as they might. But the *madness* can be overpowering, compelling those who love most to extravagant self-sacrifice. Such is the *madness* of those who love deeply in the manner of the Serving King. These are those who will not rest until every loved one has found freedom from the insanity of sin. Chase on, the party is about to start...

Day 40

LIFE INTERRUPTED...

"A man who was merely a man and said the sort of things Jesus said would not be a great moral teacher. He would either be a lunatic – on a level with the man who says he is a poached egg – or else he would be the Devil of Hell. You must make your choice. Either this man was, and is, the Son of God; or else a madman or something worse." —C. S. Lewis

To them belong the patriarchs, and from their race, according to the flesh, is the Christ, who is God over all, blessed forever. Amen.
(Romans 9:5)

The many, distracted by life's mundane barrage of activity, rarely take time to engage the Serving King, to listen carefully to His proclamations, to attentively evaluate His challenges to trek ever deeper into His ways of *'being and doing'*. Nor does the Serving King mandate attentiveness by the masses as they scurry here and there in their brave attempt to find meaning and purpose apart from Him. The masses simply endure the life of distraction, ignorant of the opportunity to sit at the feet of *the Christ, who is God over all*. And they are not the first to be so distracted. Life distracts all persons from a *life interrupted*.

But distracted and ignorant you are not. Yours is a life *interrupted*, a moment at the feet of *the Christ*, a time for decision, an opportunity missed by the masses as they scurry by. And you are not the first to pause, to see Him for who He really is, to genuinely comprehend the significance unfolding across your mind. Nor are you the last. You are simply part of the throng of those whose lives were *interrupted* by the presence of the Serving King. He continues to interrupt. It is what He does.

And with *life interrupted* comes opportunity, the privilege to seize the moment, to disengage from the scurrying masses, to change course and chase after the Serving King. But this chase is rarely mandatory; rather, it is an invitation to come along, to join the few seizing the advantage of *seeing* what so many others have missed. This is the ultimate advantage in life, the privilege of stepping into the lineage of those captured by the attention of the Serving King. You are not alone in this *life interrupted*. Pay attention in this moment of pause. The treadmill of life will begin its rotation soon enough. And when it does, chase on after the Serving King...

Day 41

BLOODLINES...

"There is no caste in blood." —Edwin Arnold

But it is not as though the word of God has failed. For not all who are descended from Israel belong to Israel, and not all are children of Abraham because they are his offspring, but
"Through Isaac shall your offspring be named."
(Romans 9:6-7)

E very parent longs for the reality of *spiritual grandchildren*, birthrights extended through the simplicity of *bloodlines*, an inheritance easily transferred to loved ones. But no such access exists into the Kingdom of God. *Bloodlines* never provide salvific inheritance, instead, only salvific opportunities of the grandest kind. But it is critical to never confuse opportunities with guaranteed contracts. The Kingdom of God is always relational and rarely contractual. And each person must begin their own chase after the Serving King.

But moderns love contracts of every kind, promises written in blood, mandates guaranteeing this or that in the days to come. And so, the many approach the chase after the Serving King as merely another contract, signed and delivered, guaranteeing those embarking on the trek an everlasting spot in the lineage of the King. Such was the foolishness of those thinking *bloodlines* sufficient in sustaining a vital relationship to the King. But alas, "There is no caste in blood."

The novice, inexperienced in His ways of *'being and doing'*, often meanders off the trail of the Serving King, destined for the pain and chaos awaiting those who drift into the wilderness. Fear not, the good Shepherd always comes looking for the meandering soul. Thus, the invitation to return to the path of the Serving King: A glorious reunion.

But the fool, confusing *following* with *contract*, often intentionally deviates from the path of the Serving King, destined as well for the pain and chaos of the wilderness. And the good Shepherd comes looking for this lost sheep as well. And again, the invitation to return to the path of the Serving King is extended. But the fool, convinced the *contract* in tact, waves away the Serving King and deeper into the wilderness goes the fool. And so, the words of the Serving King come echoing into the wilderness, "Not everyone who says to me, 'Lord, Lord,' will enter the kingdom of heaven..." (Matthew 7:21). Chase on while you can...

Day 42

PROMISES...

*"We are acceptable with God not because we have obeyed, or because
we have promised to give up things, but because of the death of Christ,
and in no other way." —Oswald Chambers*

*This means that it is not the children of the flesh who are the children of God,
but the children of the promise are counted as offspring.
(Romans 9:8)*

The chase after the Serving King is filled with *promises*, some kept, many broken, all from a well-intentioned heart. And the novice chaser is often tempted to live in the illusion of self-sufficiency before God, faithfulness in chasing well, obedience in the present moment. But God's acceptance of those chasing after the Serving King has no basis for the trek itself; rather, it is the *promise* of the Son to stand beside those who respond to the invitation to follow the Serving King. He *promised* to give His life as a ransom for the many, and to that promise He has been faithful and true.

And it is the fulfilled promised to lay down His life for the sake of the many which provides the basis for the Father's acceptance of all those who follow the Serving King into the presence of God. The *promise* has been fulfilled in the life and death of the Serving King, and with it the *children of the promise* rise to the surface. Those who chase in faith are the children of the promise.

The children of the promise are the children of faith, those who have responded well to the call of the Son to come and follow. Their treks after the Serving King are so very different, rooted in unique personal encounters with the Serving King, each uniquely powerful and creative. No two are ever the same. But His *promise* to stand with those who respond in faith to His invitation remains consistent across the ages. Only His promise to stand with each trekker provides access to the presence of the King.

Hence, they come in various sizes and shapes, various ways of chasing after the King, patterns unique to each calling. The only constant is the *promise* of the Serving King to stand with each and every *child of the promise*. Chase on into the promise of the Serving King...

Day 43

FOLLOW THROUGH...

"I can give you a six-word formula for success: Think things through—then follow through." —Eddie Rickenbacker

For the statement of the promise is this: "At this time I will return and Sarah will have a son. And not only this, but also when Rebecca conceived children by one man, Isaac our father—
(Romans 9:9-10)

Moderns, desperate for follow through, surrendered the value of a person's promise, their word, long ago. In its place, contracts of every kind, each carefully worded in an effort to create follow through, the missing link within the human experience. And still the courts are filled with broken contracts of all kinds. Even contracts fail to guarantee the value of the individuals signing on the dotted line. Follow through still the longed for dimension of human commitments of every kind. Little wonder moderns struggle as they attempt to embrace God's follow through.

Success has never been depended on words alone; instead, it has always been the follow through ushering in success. And God, unlike those attempting to trust Him, always follows through. So Sarah and Rebecca discovered as the promise of God soon became the reality to which His promise pointed. The words of God always become the realities to which they point.

For those who hear the promises of God, the decision remains, shall I step into the reality God has promised or shall I cautiously wait and see? Those who wait, too fearful to step into God's promised reality, soon discover God waits for no person. Instead, God moves forward with those brave enough to trust the words of God that will soon become cherished realities. And so, the promise of God that there are those coming who will indeed embrace God's promises.

So comes the opportunity for those who now hear God to step into the reality arriving just around the bend. But understand, God often proclaims new realities into lives long ago abandoned as old and barren. God proclaims new life into those who have not abandoned faith, have not abandoned dreams, still believing God to bring new life to those courageous enough to embrace God's follow through. And rest assured, God always thinks things through, and having done so, always follows through. Chase on...

Day 44

PURPOSE...

"Learn to get in touch with the silence within yourself, and know that everything in life has purpose. There are no mistakes, no coincidences, all events are blessings given to us to learn from." —Elisabeth Kubler-Ross

...though they were not yet born and had done nothing either good or bad—in order that God's purpose of election might continue, not because of works but because of Him who calls— she was told, "The older will serve the younger." (Romans 9:11-12)

Moderns love the concept of *random,* a meaningless sequence of events, unleashing nothing more than mere chance upon the lives of those scurrying across the globe. And *random* is purposeless as it dances across the ages, never concerned with productivity or intention, recklessly crisscrossing this way and that. The naive, thinking *random* a manageable nuisance, works hard to stay clear of it, giving it a wide berth, avoiding *random chance* whenever possible. But staying clear of *random* is a fool's game, and, sooner or later, *random* touches every life, often painfully and without purpose. Such is the greatest pain of all.

But those chasing after the Serving King soon discover the intentionality of the King's path, the interconnectedness of each and every aspect of life, the absolute absence of purposeless *random.* In its place rises up a profound new understanding concerning the *everything has purpose in life.* Also, comes the discovery of *purpose* beyond the *good or bad* of each person's life, the intentionality of God in unleashing *salvific* significance into every moment of *random,* "...that God's purpose of election might continue."

And *purpose* is the key to life, the foundation of sanity in a world filled with seemingly meaningful chaos, the glue giving life purpose and direction. Those chasing after the Serving King soon develop eyes capable of seeing *God's purpose* in the midst of the *random* unfolding in the events of every day. And God offers no greater gift than the ability to see *purpose* in the midst of the seeming chaos. But rest assured, there will be days when the specifics of *purpose* will remain unseen, yet undisclosed as the "...older will serve the younger." Nonetheless, the "ah-ha" will come for those who look deeper, patiently waiting for clarity to appear. Indeed, there are no meaningless moments for those chasing after the Serving King...

Day 45

COULD HAVE BEENS...

"A pessimist sees the difficulty in every opportunity; an optimist sees the opportunity in every difficulty." —Winston Churchhill

...she was told, "The older will serve the younger."
As it is written, "Jacob I loved, but Esau I hated."
(Romans 9:12-13)

Those chasing after the Serving King soon discover the scope of God's creation, a landscape littered with a vast array of alternatives, places and times that *could have been* but simply are not. And the novice chaser will be tempted to fantasize about another's chase, opportunities never offered along the trail as the Serving King leads into the reality designed precisely for each trekker. Concern for *fairness regarding* others and self becomes a nagging nuisance in the quest after the Serving King. Still the novice chases on.

But farther down the path, the question of fairness in the swirling mass of *could have beens* begins to gnaw at those chasing after the Serving King. Fairness whispers its concerns in the ear of those walking closely behind the Serving King. And so comes the inevitable question, "What about Esau?" Esaus abound in life, fellow lost wanderers whose lives seem void of *could have beens*, opportunities missed or, worse yet, *could have beens* never seeming to appear. So the novice pauses to look closer at life's *could have beens*.

But chasers soon realize their limited vision, void of both past and future, stuck in the limited scope of the present moment, a moment disconnected from previous *could have beens* and every future *could have been*. And with such a limited field of vision comes the realization of an inability to answer the questions of *fairness*. Such questions inevitably are answered only at the throne of the King.

But for the persistent questioner, sooner or later, there comes the proverbial "mind your own business" echoing down the hallway from the Father's throne of grace. It is not a proclamation of *fairness*; rather, a simple decree of sovereignty by Him who answers to no one. And the Serving King points to His cross and all questions of fairness fade. Chase on until fairness meets you at the throne of the King...

Day 46

PERSPECTIVE...

"If you are neutral in situations of injustice, you have chosen the side of the oppressor. If an elephant has its foot on the tail of a mouse and you say that you are neutral, the mouse will not appreciate your neutrality."
—Desmond Tutu

What shall we say then? Is there injustice on God's part? By no means!
(Romans 9:14)

Elephants, intentional or not, standing on the tail of a mouse create immediate images, each begging for an answer to the proverbial question, "Why?" And the *why* dictates all kinds of responses toward the elephant upon the tail. And the mouse most interested of all.

The novice chaser determined to find *justice* often scolds the elephant, persistent to free the mouse from such an oppressor. And, indeed, the elephant could be a cruel oppressor tormenting the poor mouse. But the novice's perspective is limited in so many ways, rendering the poor novice ill-suited for the role of scolding the elephant upon the tail.

A deeper look often reveals mitigating circumstances concerning the elephant and the mouse. The elephant, towering above the mouse, sees a world the mouse knows nothing off, full of turmoil and danger around countless unseen corners. Just ahead, lying stealthily in the tall grass, waits the hungry snake confident of the coming meal, the mouse just around the bend. So the elephant stands on the tail of the mouse waiting patiently for the corner to clear, safe passage just a moment away. All the while the mouse complains.

Those chasing on the heels of the Serving King soon discover to trust the *perspective* of the Serving King, towering as He does above the mice following His carefully laid-out course. And you will be tempted along the way to scold the Serving King for this or that stepped upon tail, but eventually comes the understanding of *perspective*, the panoramic vision of the Serving King. Likewise comes the realization of *purpose* in every unfolding event as those chasing along experience all life has to offer in the path after the Serving King. And so comes another causal question, "Why didn't you step on my tail?" Chase on until your perspective clears...

Day 47

RICHEST FRUIT...

"I have always found that mercy bears richer fruits than strict justice."
—Abraham Lincoln

For He says to Moses, "I will have mercy on whom I have mercy,
and I will have compassion on whom I have compassion."
(Romans 9:15)

The power of *mercy* rises up out of its unexpected arrival in the midst of certain doom and judgment, unleashing its power toward those whom *mercy* has set free, those whose lives have been spared the impending execution. Once touched by *mercy* in the midst of dire circumstances, life can never be the same. Such is the transformative power of *mercy,* the *richest of fruit,* the unexpected fruit.

But the crowd, suspect of the power of *mercy,* murmurs as it shuffles away, frustrated by justice abated yet again, fearful the spared life will return to its chaotic and destructive path. So the murmuring crowd agonizes over the reign of *mercy,* longing for a promised redemption, fearful it will never arrive on the heels of *mercy,* believing justice the much-needed solution to the sin of humanity. But they are wrong. Mercy is the power of God unleashed upon a lost and dying world. It bears richer fruit than mere justice.

However, those chasing after the Serving King know firsthand the *richest fruit of mercy,* living testimonies to the power of *mercy* in a life touched in the midst of certain doom and judgment. They understand the *will of God* extending *mercy* to those most undeserving, having already tasted the glory of *mercy* at their own trial, their own dramatic moment, an unexpected face-to-face with the King of Kings. They implicitly trust the power of mercy in a land of impending doom.

Released from the imminent doom, those *graced by mercy* can do nothing less than bear fruit in response to the nourishment of *mercy.* Indeed, theirs is the *richest fruit* of all. And so, the power of *mercy* sweeps over a land of dread, offering hope to the hopeless, life to the lifeless, redemption of the highest kind. This is the power of God for those who chase on...

Day 48

UNINITIATED...

"If you want to make people mad, preach law. If you want to make them really, really mad, preach grace" —Tullian Tchividjian

So then it depends not on human will or exertion, but on God, who has mercy.
(Romans 9:16)

The *fool,* resistant to the proclamation of God, exerts great effort in establishing criteria for earning the grace of God, much-needed *mercy* evading all trying-hard persons. In doing so, the *fool* seeks to cage God, insisting God operate within reasonable guidelines established by the well-meaning *fool.* The offered criteria, noble in so many ways, often full of compassion and justice, ways of 'being and doing' reflecting the *'being and doing'* of God, makes no impression on Him who extends mercy. Only God establishes the criteria, *if any,* for receiving mercy. The best the *fool* can do is seek to comprehend the criteria for *mercy,* if indeed any can be found trailing behind Him who has mercy, Him who was crucified for your sake.

And nothing may be more humbling in life than the recognition of God's sovereignty in executing *mercy* according to His own intention and purpose, independent of human will or exertion. Hence, there are no avenues by which human will can claim the necessity of God's *mercy* being exercised. Mercy is entirely in the will of God, yes, entirely the *will of God* and extended as God sees fit.

Still, the novice trekker, inexperienced in the ways of mercy, the unpredictability of grace, often attempts to rationalize the pathway to *mercy,* the criteria by which God must extend mercy to those trailing behind Serving King. But in the end, all one ever discovers is the behavior of those who have been graced by *mercy;* never the criteria by which *mercy* must be extended.

Tragically, the *uninitiated* often confuse the behavior of those graced by *mercy* as the avenue to *mercy.* Convinced they have found the path to *mercy, the uninitiated* often mimic the behavior of those so touched, thinking they too have found *mercy.* But alas, *...it depends not on human will or exertion.* That is the fool's game. Mercy comes by faith in those chasing on...

Day 49

INDIGNANT...

"Do not weep; do not wax indignant. Understand." —Baruch Spinoza

For the Scripture says to Pharaoh, "For this very purpose I have raised you up,
that I might show my power in you, and that My name might be
proclaimed in all the earth."
(Romans 9:17)

The fool, those most committed to standing tall in opposition to the revelation of the King, suffer the most indignant fate of all, every act of deviance embraced by the King for His own purposes, intricate pieces of the redemptive process. So the King proclaims to the king of fools, "For this very purpose..." It is the ultimate futility of life, the grand folly, ever glorifying the King even in the act of deviance and rebellion. So the *indignant* fate of Pharaoh.

And so comes the announcement of God that even those who oppose Him must play a vital role in the unfolding Kingdom of God. Some would be actors, even a starring role in the grand drama playing out from the hand of God. And for the very few, those whose defiance takes on an intensity of the highest kind, God reinforces their rebellion, ensuring no reconsideration at the highest moment of the King's purposes, the zenith of rebellion's futility as the purpose of God unfolds, precisely as God envisions.

Thus, modern Pharaohs rise to their performance, ever ready to step into their leading role, eloquent in rebellion, persistent in their malicious pursuit of those embracing the call of the Serving King. They, too, shine in their performance, dogged in their chase, ready to cross their own modern *dead sea,* only to discover the tragic truth, "For this purpose I have raised you up..."

In that climatic moment, they will face the temptation to *weep or wax indignant.* But there is so little time left in their concluding scene, time slipping away as the grand drama draws to a close. This is the moment to *understand,* to leave *indignity* behind, to embrace the King before the play is over. It is the final act of this unfolding drama. Embrace a new "For this very purpose I have raised you up." Regardless of the chosen ending, His name will be lifted up, even in those who do not chase on...

Day 50

MORAL APTITUDE...

"A dark cloud is no sign that the sun has lost his light; and dark black convictions are no arguments that God has laid aside His mercy."
—Charles Spurgeon

So then He has mercy on whomever He wills,
and He hardens whomever He wills.
(Romans 9:18)

Moderns, confident in their moral aptitude, are quick to discern what is good, pleasing, and acceptable. A confidence so profound few hesitate in making each and every pronouncement available for all the world to see. And, oh, the joy of social media, the poster board of all such discernments. Declarations of every kind, each proclaiming the wisdom of the modern sage, confidently announcing the proper recipients of mercy or grace. Like Pharaoh before them, usurping the role properly assigned to God and God alone.

But like so many 'pharaohs' before them, moderns soon retreat as the righteous Judge appears over the horizon. All bravado vanquished at the feet of the King, the sound of His righteous decrees echoing across the land, all pretense vanishing in His presence, valor but a distant memory. The charade now over, righteousness restored, His declarations the only ones that matter.

Eyes now fully open, understanding finally arriving, moderns join Pharaoh in a momentary change of heart. Who can persist in such folly standing in the presence of the Serving King. The inevitable now crashing down, understanding and insight abounding, modern pharaohs join the Pharaoh of old relinquishing proclamations of every kind. Wisdom suddenly abounding.

But God cannot be mocked nor fooled, nor has God been oblivious to the motivation behind the sudden change of heart. The fool's true colors have already been revealed. The leopard's spots clearly visible to all who are paying attention. The destiny already earned. So God ignores the temporary change of heart returning the fool back to his true colors, his old ways of 'being and doing'. God hardens the blackened heart to its true color, ignoring the pretense of the present moment. God can never be fooled by the fool's moment of accommodation. Back to his true colors he will go. Chase on...

Day 51

ARMS OF DESTINY...

*"Gladly we desire to make other men perfect, but we will not
amend our own fault."* —Thomas a Kempis

*You will say to me then, "Why does He still find fault?
For who can resist His will?"
(Romans 9:19)*

There is a moment for all persons in which *intention of the human heart* becomes *destiny*, an unavoidable fate waiting for mere *intention of the human heart* to arrive in the *arms of destiny,* God's will. And like all moments, each moment is nothing more, nothing less, than God's will impregnated with His purposes. Hence, the question of each moment is not "What is it?" Clearly, it is God's will, but, rather, "How did it come to be?"

The novice trekker, anxious to rid oneself of all responsibility, raises the timeless rhetorical question, "Why does He still find fault?' Hoping, instead, for a thorough whitewashing of personal responsibility, a comforting reply of "He doesn't." But such is never the case. The *intention of the human heart* always plays a critical role in the destiny soon to become God's will.

Such is the life of Pharaoh as he finally arrives in the arms of destiny, God's will, stepping into the *purpose* that has awaited him from the beginning of time. Long before God hardened his heart, the *intention of the human heart*, Pharaoh's heart, laid claim to the path awaiting Pharaoh's destiny, the will of God. Pharaoh, blinded by the *intention of the human heart,* steps into the awaiting will of God, "...but Pharaoh hardened his heart this time also, and did not let the people go" *(Exodus 8:32).*

But there is more at work here than simply *the intention of the human heart.* God is equally at work initiating *destiny,* mandating a future that cannot be averted, His will unfolding in the present moment, embracing the *intention of the human heart.* "But the Lord hardened the heart of Pharaoh, and he did not listen to them, as the Lord had spoken to Moses" (Exodus 9:12). For indeed, who can resist His will as it embraces the *intention of the human heart?* Chase on into the destiny of your own heart...

Day 52

OTHERWISE...

"God is a God of purpose. He doesn't wake-up and start dabbling into things; He doesn't practice trial and error. His ways are sure, they may be low but they are always sure." —Jaachynma N.E. Agu

But who are you, O man, to answer back to God?
Will what is molded say to its molder, "Why have you made me like this?"
(Romans 9:20)

Self-awareness is a startling moment ushering in a keen sense of independence, separation from every other aspect of the creation. As René Descartes noted, "It is the grand awakening in which one becomes vividly cognizant of 'I am' and 'I am not you'". More startling, however, is the realization things could have been *otherwise*, different than they are, reality of another kind. It is self-awareness of a special kind, the recognition of *design and purpose* independent of self, the cradle in which self-awareness awakens. And so arrives the probing question, "Why have You (God) made me like this?"

The *fool* spends countless hours mourning *what is* and lusting for what could have been, the *otherwise.* The question serves more as a complaint, informing God of one's displeasure with the current state of affairs. So arrives the mantra of the masses, a constant droning about what should have been, could have been.

But those chasing after the Serving King begin to embrace the question as an authentic search for life's meaning, a reason for *'being and doing'* in the quest after the Serving King. The question becomes an announcement of understanding, recognition of intentionality in the creative hand of God, abandonment of *otherwise*.

With the abandonment of *otherwise* comes a final embracing of the *I am*, just as God intended, a life filled with meaning and purpose. And for those chasing deepest into the quest after the Serving King comes the realization of intentionality and purpose, even when in the midst of self-generated pain and chaos. And so, God lays claim to every dimension of His creation. God is indeed a God of purpose, even when allowing the creation to self-determine, to self-destroy. There is no trial and error in the Kingdom of God, only the unfolding of divine intentionality. Chase on into God's intention designed especially for you...

Day 53

USED...

"What we need to do is always lean into the future; when the world changes around you and when it changes against you—what used to be a tail wind is now a head wind—you have to lean into that and figure out what to do because complaining isn't a strategy." —Jeff Bezos

Has the potter no right over the clay, to make out of the same lump one vessel for honorable use and another for dishonorable use?
(Romans 9:21)

Novices, those just starting out on the chase after the Serving King, often make false assumptions concerning the *kind* of trek the journey will be. Visions of grandeur often fill the mind generating grand expectations for the days ahead, peaceful strolls through flowered valleys in the warmth of a spring day. But sooner or later, and only at the King's discretion, life finds its way into the mountains, difficult trials, filled with unexpected peril. So go the plans of mice and men.

The novice, unprepared for *dishonorable use,* often grumbles, "This is not how I planned on the King using my life." And so comes the sudden realization this journey, planned long before anyone signed on for the chase, is beyond the control of any single adventurer. You are also part of the grand plan, God's purposes unfolding in every detail of your life, whether 'honorable' or 'dishonorable'.

Further, the trek has far-reaching implications, way beyond mere individual consequences and ramifications. Hence, complaining, the ever-present temptation, *isn't a strategy;* rather, the murmurings of those who refuse to *lean into* the *use* the Potter has prepared. But whether one *leans into* the Potter's mold or not, the Potter's desires take shape, ushering in the Potter's purposes.

In the end, every piece of the *lump* has a purpose in the Potter's creation. No piece insignificant, no miscellaneous leftovers. Every bit of the *lump* will be *used* precisely as the Potter has intended to bring about His purposes. The key is to recognize the joy of being *used* for the purposes of the King. And, in doing so, the words of the Serving King ring true for those whose *use* was not as desirable as others, "But many who are first shall be last. And the last shall be first" (Mark 10:31). Lean into the shape the Potter has prepared and embrace His purposes as you chase on...

Day 54

WHY?

"He who has a why to live can bear almost any how." —*Friedrich Nietzsche*

What if God, desiring to show His wrath and to make known His power, has endured with much patience vessels of wrath prepared for destruction...
(Romans 9:22)

Moderns, like every generation, have long struggled with the *why* of those parts of the creation appearing to contribute so little to the chase after the Serving King. *Why* does God allow the chaos within the creation to continue on its destructive course? The question expresses the realization things could be different should God choose to make them different. God is sovereign in each and every moment, even this very moment. Hence, the question, "Why?" Or as many have expressed, "The problem of evil in a world created and sustained by God." And the complexities of *why* are multifaceted, embracing a wide range of possibilities, each playing an essential role in the comprehensive purpose of God.

But *endurance* is a two-way street. The creation must endure the consequences of its broken constituent parts inflicting pain and chaos into the system. Likewise, God *endures* the brokenness within His creation precisely because even the brokenness has purpose in the Kingdom of God. God uses every piece in every moment.

Thus, even that which must be endured has a productive dimension enhancing the reconciliation God is bringing about for every aspect of the creation. Even those *vessels* refusing to embrace the reconciliation offered by God will still be used by God in a redemptive manner. Specifically, even those vessels refusing to embrace reconciliation are *prepared* to assist in manifesting the *wrath and power* of God as redemption unfolds. No piece of the creation is left out of the redemptive process.

And so, God does indeed desire to embrace every piece of His creation in the redemptive process. There is no opting out of redemption as it unfolds. The only decision left is the role one will play. The *why* of your life clearly sets the cast for the *how* that is about to unfold. Choose this day the destination awaiting you as you chase on...

Day 55

PREPARED…

"Many promising reconciliations have broken down because while both parties come prepared to forgive, neither party come prepared to be forgiven."
—Charles Williams

…in order to make known the riches of His glory for vessels of mercy, which He has prepared beforehand for glory.
(Romans 9:23)

The decision to chase after the Serving King is always preceded by an act toward God for forgiveness, a response to God's movement toward us *while we were yet still sinners* (Roman 5:8). And those who seek forgiveness must first become aware of the need for *mercy, forgiveness*, in all its forms. Preparing to be forgiven sounds easy enough, and, occasionally, it is, but rarely does forgiveness come easy in the presence of God. God's standard, often unseen and unnoticed until in His presence, is incredibly high, mandating perfection from the creation. Hence, those who come must be *prepared* to seek forgiveness across an incredibly large spectrum of possibilities within perfection. And with each step deeper into the chase after the Serving King comes the awareness of how much forgiveness is genuinely required by God. There is no *trivial* sin in the Kingdom of God.

Tragically, many come toward God expecting a two-way exchange, forgiveness from God and for God, "…He hardens whomever He wills." You will say to me then, "Why does He still find fault? For who can resist His will?" (Romans 9:19) And so, the pauper's prayer of forgiveness, "I forgive you God for making this mess!" The breakdown in negotiations becomes clear as the offending party demands God to seek forgiveness as well, an exchange only the fool would expect. And wait the fool will for an everlasting moment in time.

But there is no shortage of mercy from God, even toward those who think God guilty of creating the mess. Instead, God continues to move in mercy toward those determined to set God straight. It is the way of God to move in mercy toward the entirety of His creation. Only those most persistent in resisting the mercy of God lose access to His mercy. Others quickly receive the glory prepared beforehand for His vessels of mercy. Chase on into His mercy…

Day 56

STRANGE BEDFELLOWS...

"Religion acquaints a man with strange bedfellows."
—a modified Shakespeare

...even us whom He has called, not from the Jews only
but also from the Gentiles?
(Romans 9:24)

The early stages of the chase after the Serving King are often filled with expected *bedfellows*, folks acting and thinking in expected ways, common ways, familiar ways. And, oh, the comfort found in chasing alongside *like-minded* folks. Predictability is comforting in so many ways. So the persistent gathering of the *like-minded*.

But the King is never satisfied with the gathering of the *like-minded,* cloned and honed to exacting dimensions, mirrored images as the crowd shuffles along in common tempo. No, this King seeks an endless array of chasers, individuals radically committed to chasing after the Serving King but dressed in identities from a vast array of peoples and places, walking in a cadence from another place, another way. This is the God of the *Gentiles* too.

Nonetheless, the crowd, used to only *common bedfellows,* is slow to receive these *Gentiles* from another land, another way of *'being and doing'* in the specific calling of the King. These are sheep from different pasture led by the Master Shepherd, the Serving King, fellow heirs in the Kingdom of God. They, too, have received *mercy,* are *vessels of mercy,* just as the other sheep.

So the Kingdom of God is the gathering of the *strange bedfellows,* sometimes *very strange bedfellows,* each stunned to discover a *bedfellow* of another kind, equally engaged in the chase after the Serving King. And most stunning of all may be the realization of the Serving King's love for these *strange bedfellows* He has brought to the sheep pen, the pasture where God's people gather to rest in the presence of the Serving King. Those longest in the chase after the Serving King have come to expect *strange bedfellows* in the Kingdom of God. It is the way of the Serving King. And, of course, they have come to understand they were once the *strangest bedfellows* of all as they chased on after the Serving King...

Day 57

ALIENS...

"We of alien looks or words must stick together." —C.J. Sansom

*As indeed He says in Hosea, "Those who were not My people
I will call My people, and her who was not beloved I will call beloved.
And in the very place where it was said to them, 'You are not My people,'
there they will be called 'Sons of the Living God.'"*
(Romans 9:25-26)

The arrival of the *aliens*, those who walk and talk in ways unfamiliar to you, always creates awkwardness in the crowd chasing after the Serving King. And those previously engaged in the trek, familiar with the terrain and the crowd, immediately assume the *aliens* will learn soon enough. And some do. Some quickly fall in step with those trailing after the Serving King.

But there comes that moment when certain *aliens* fail to mimic the cadence of the crowd and still remain hot on the heels of the Serving King. More alarming, the realization the Serving King loves these *aliens*, even calls these *aliens* His very own, even His *beloved*. But most alarming is His embracing of their way of *'being and doing'*, their way of chasing after the Serving King. And then comes the stunning proclamation concerning the *aliens*, robust and profound, ringing in the ears of the crowd, "Sons of the Living God!"

Aliens, those different than the previous crowd, have often been rejected by the crowd, declared too *alien* to be sheep of His pen. And yet, there they are, delivered by the Serving King, declared "Sons of the living God." So comes the discovery of *others* in the Kingdom of God. And, perhaps, the genius of the Kingdom of God becomes most visible in the gathering of the *alien tribes* all strolling behind the Serving King, each suspicious of the others, wondering if those *aliens* are really part of the Shepherd's flock.

But there are a *few* in every tribe, those who recognize the gathering of the *aliens* is the genius of the Kingdom of God, the hidden accessibility for the masses, the *mystery made known of the Kingdom of God*. And a bold few in every clan whisper to the others, "We of alien looks or words must stick together." Understand, more are on the way who are equally chasing on...

Day 58

THE REMNANT...

"If your descent is from heroic sires, show in your life a remnant of their fires."
—*Nicolas Boileau-Despreaux*

And Isaiah cries out concerning Israel: "Though the number of the sons of Israel be as the sand of the sea, only a remnant of them will be saved, for the Lord will carry out His sentence upon the earth fully and without delay."
(Romans 9:27-28)

The chase after the Serving King often draws a crowd, sometimes a very large crowd, if the terrain remains pleasant enough. And many within the crowd, having long ago lost sight of the Serving King, will anticipate an enjoyable destination as the crowd shuffles along. Such is the life of those who confuse chasing after the Serving King with hanging out in the crowd. Sadly, the crowd often never notices the King has moved on.

The confusion arrives only when the Serving King is gone from sight, and all that remains is the crowd talking about the Serving King, reminiscing about the *good old days* of chasing after the Serving King. The stories, delightful and entertaining, continue to draw larger and larger crowds, like the *sands of the sea,* countless people in search of safer pastures. The comfort of the masses is heart-warming, reassuring all who mingle of the safety found in the crowd. But, sooner or later, comes the realization of the absence of the Serving King, nowhere to be found in the mass of humanity, the crowd having meandered off course long ago. Still, the comfort of the crowd seduces the many to shuffle along anyway, King or no King.

The remnant, those wise enough to never lose sight of the Serving King, left long ago as well, hot on the trail of the Serving King, determined to keep Him within eyesight. The remnant has no concern for the crowd diminishing in the distance with every step. They long ago decided to chase after the Serving King regardless of the cost, in isolation if need be, ever pursuing the Serving King. They are the heirs of a *heroic sire,* and His fire burns in their loins. They cannot be distracted by the crowd. They are the remnant, faithful to His calling, never losing sight of the Serving King in the midst of the many as they chase on...

Day 59

HOLD ON…

"Faith, in the sense in which I am here using the word, is the art of holding on to things your reason has once accepted, in spite of your changing moods."
—C.S. Lewis

What shall we say, then? That Gentiles who did not pursue righteousness have attained it, that is, a righteousness that is by faith…
(Romans 9:30)

T he chase after the Serving King is often a quest for *righteousness,* a right and proper way of *'being and doing',* the intuitive goal for all those in pursuit of Him. And the novice, full of enthusiasm and optimism, still days away from the agony of defeat, leaps into the quest with reckless abandon, confident of the transformation to come. But the quest for *righteousness,* a proper way of *'being and doing',* honorable and admirable as it may be, always, yes always, ends in utter failure and despair.

And in the moment of failure, *changing moods* will sweep across the landscape of emotions, often threatening the chase itself. But *righteousness* is never attained by the efforts of well-intentioned souls; rather, it is received by *faith,* borrowed from the Serving King. It is never the domain of those chasing after the Serving King. *Righteousness* can only be received, never produced by the gallant efforts of those chasers *trying hard* to be *righteous* for the glory of the Serving King. And so comes the discovery of the necessity of *righteousness that is by faith.*

But *failure* to be *righteous* is not without victories, glorious improvement, even new ways of *'being and doing'* reflecting the ways of the Serving King. These new ways of *'being and doing'* can never be the *righteousness* mandated by the King. Only the Son can manufacture such *righteousness.*

Still, these new ways of *'being and doing'* are the sweet fruit of those pursuing the *righteousness* that can never be obtained. It is a pleasing aroma filling the nostrils of God. But it is only for those who *hold on* to the quest in spite of the inherent failure, the inability to attain the necessary perfection. The quest for *righteousness* is the inevitable journey for those who have received the *righteousness that is by faith.* It is they who chase on…

Day 60

DEFEAT...

"We have fought this fight as long, and as well as we know how. We have been defeated. For us as a Christian people, there is now but one course to pursue. We must accept the situation." —Robert E. Lee

...but that Israel who pursued a law that would lead to righteousness did not succeed in reaching that law. Why? Because they did not pursue it by faith, but as if it were based on works. They have stumbled over the stumbling stone...
(Romans 9:31-32)

Defeat is a horrible moment, especially when the fight has been *as long and as well as we know how.* Such is the agony of those striving with determined hearts for *righteousness* coming from obedience to the law. And no person seriously engaged in the pursuit of *righteousness, 'being and doing'* in the manner of the Serving King, ever succeeds. The pursuit cannot be accomplished. The quest for righteousness by *works of the law* always ends in *defeat.* And yet, the dream of righteousness, proper *'being and doing',* remains in the hearts of those chasing after the Serving King. Thus, *for us as a Christian people, there is now but one course to pursue: we must accept the situation,* the unaccomplish-able task in the trek after the Serving King.

Many, destined to never measure up to the stature of the Serving King, yet thrilled to discover the *righteousness of faith,* grace in the midst of failure, simply sit down and wait for the Serving King to return. Theirs is the cruelest *defeat* of all. Destined for failure, secure in grace, wallowing in the muck, content to bask in *defeat* while waiting for the glory to come.

But there are some, perhaps, a very few, who *stumble over the stumbling stone* and rise again, now fully aware of the failure to come. Yet, seeing the *stumbling stone* moving down the trail, still dare to continue to trek after Him, determined to seek *righteousness,* to follow His way of *'being and doing',* knowing all the while, this is a battle that cannot be won, a victory unattainable, a bridge too far. Still they chase on.

Their pursuit is no quest for *worthiness* in the presence of the King. Only the *righteousness of faith* can gain access to the righteousness of the Son. No, this is a quest of another kind, to simply be like the Beloved who leads the defeated as they chase on...

Day 61

HARD CHARGERS...

"We all serve God inevitably, but it makes a great difference whether you serve like Judas or serve like John." —C.S. Lewis

Behold, I am laying in Zion a stone of stumbling, and a rock of offense; and whoever believes in Him will not be put to shame.
(Romans 9:33)

Any declaration of ineptitude offends, and none more so than the proclamation of Gospel, the necessity of grace, even for those trying their very best. It is those *hard chargers*, making every effort to please the Serving King, who stumble hardest on His declaration of ineptitude and the necessity of a Savior. His is not a declaration of *making up the difference* for all who have exerted great effort in the chase after the Serving King; rather, a nullifying of every effort but His. It is they, those hard-working folks, who stumble the most over the Serving King and His doctrine of grace.

More disheartening for *hard chargers* is the proclamation of acceptance toward the slackers, those who make little or no effort in chasing after the Serving King, those who simply *believe in Him* and receive freedom from shame, entrance into the Kingdom of God.

But *hard chargers* soon realize we all serve God inevitably, each playing a vital role in the unfolding plan of God. And for those *hard chargers* who rise up from their encounter with the *stone of stumbling* comes a grand realization, the privilege of obedience and the fruit therein. Obedience provides no salvific benefit or enhancement, only the *stone of stumbling* can provide the righteousness needed for salvation; nonetheless, *hard chargers* soon discover the fruit of obedience, the *abundant life made possible by those charging hard into His ways of 'being and doing'.*

Obedience is no added burden for those charging hard into the trek after the Serving King. To the contrary, it is the grand privilege of *hard charging*, the unexpected fringe benefit for those freed from the necessity of earning their way into the Kingdom of God. Obedience is the sweetest fruit for those who have finally risen up from their encounter with the *stone of stumbling.* They will indeed chase on...

Day 62

ULTIMATE CONCERN…

"Concern should drive us into action and not into a depression."
—Pythagoras

Brothers, my heart's desire and prayer to God for
them is that they may be saved.
(Romans 10:1)

Concern for others is an inevitable consequence of chasing after the Serving King. His passion becomes their passion. And *concern*, authentic interest in the well-being of those not yet on the trek, drives those so *concerned* into action, redemptive action on the behalf of others. Hence, the Serving King's journey to the cross. And well-intentioned followers of the King often seek their own cross, verifiable means of acting on behalf of others not yet on the trek. *Concern should drive chasers into action.*

But there is an action that ought to precede all actions. It is the preeminent action, the foundation superseding all other actions of *concern*, the *ground of being* upon which all action must rest. It is the manifestation of an *ultimate concern*. Nonetheless, foundations are difficult to establish requiring much painstaking preparatory work, grueling hours in the presence of the King. It is, of course, the work of prayer, the *ultimate concern*, time spent unleashing the power of God into the lives of those you yearn to find salvation, to join the chase after the Serving King.

Novice trekkers, too anxious in abandoning the *ultimate concern* in the solitude of the closet, race into the mission field engaging in a multitude of good works. And so, the *good works* rise up drawing the applause of many, even from those not *concerned* with the chase after the Serving King. But salvation cannot stand on any foundation but prayer, deep and solid, the bedrock upon which salvation must rest.

The many, too engaged with *busy work*, concerned only enough to remain active in the field, rarely pause long enough to demonstrate *ultimate concern*. This is the hard work of prayer, the *ultimate concern*, the most difficult of all works. Few are those engaged in *ultimate concern* as they chase on…

Day 63

ZEALOTS...

"The greatest dangers to liberty lurk in the insidious encroachment by men of zeal, well meaning but without understanding." —Louis D. Brandeis

For I bear them witness that they have a zeal for God,
but not according to knowledge.
(Romans 10:2)

Zealots, believers of the finest kind, warriors unhinged by cautioning doubt, charge into battle inspired by assurances no longer relevant. And moderns, convinced radical belief makes it true, join the zealots in proclaiming assurances rooted in rock solid belief. The problem, of course, is that believing something, anything, with all of your heart, doesn't make it true. It simply makes you a zealot. And the world continues to be filled with zealots of every kind.

But there is a zealot of the most dangerous kind, the zealot stuck in yesterday's truth unable to move forward into today's revelation. Yesterday's truth was powerful, meaningful and relevant for yesterday. Zealots know the power of yesterday's revelation, yesterday's truth. And yesterday was a glorious day as the truth of yesterday, God's revelation for yesterday brought about its intended results. Obedience unleashed the power of yesterday's revelation.

Unfortunately, the zealot often forgets to continue listening, to return to the well over and over, to replenish the bucket with today's fresh water. Instead, confident yesterday's revelation is meant for every day, the zealot stops searching for today's revelation, stuck in the truth of yesterday.

But for those determined to hear God afresh and anew, yesterday's revelation merely sets the stage for what God will say today. And today's revelation, like yesterday's, is filled with meaning and immediate relevancy. But today's revelation will require a willingness to hear again today, to open your heart and mind to the voice of God in the present moment, today's circumstances. You will be tempted to take the easier road, to dwell in yesterday's revelation, and to do so with great zeal. Alas, living in yesterday's revelation with great gusto simply makes one a zealot but not according to today's knowledge. Dare to chase on into the revelation designed especially for today...

Day 64

PAINFUL IGNORANCE...

"We can easily forgive a child who is afraid of the dark; the real tragedy of life is when men are afraid of the light." —Plato

For, being ignorant of the righteousness of God, and seeking to establish their own, they did not submit to God's righteousness. (Romans 10:3)

I gnorance, authentic unknowing, is a serious foe for the well-intentioned heart. And clearly, there is no shortage of well-intentioned, yet ignorant hearts in the quest after God. Tragically, ignorance provides no buffer for the well-intentioned as the consequences of ignorance come crashing down on those well-intentioned seekers crawling around in the dark. Tragically, innocent bystanders are equally touched by the consequences of well-intentioned ignorance. But God rarely leaves persistent seekers *in the dark,* instead offering *light* upon the trail yet ahead.

Nonetheless, *light* is often painful for eyes long accustomed to wandering around in the dark. And those exposed to the *light* often shrink away from the *light,* ill-prepared to leave the domain of darkness, patterns of living now quite comfortable for those long accustomed to the dark. No darkness more dangerous than darkness cloaked in the dim light of self-righteousness, the pretense of *good enough* for entrance into the throne room of the King.

And *light* is problematic on so many fronts for those determined to make the patterns of *dark-living* acceptable to God. But there is no hiding from the *light* of God. You simply cannot unsee what has been seen. Nor can the lighted path for today's trek be ignored as the temptation to wander down old, familiar paths lures the sighted down old, comfortable roads, ways of *'being and doing'* acceptable in the days of old, but no longer.

So comes the decision to surrender to the *light* or steadfastly refuse to yield. Many are those *afraid of the light,* unwilling to journey down paths new and unfamiliar. Indeed, *the real tragedy of life is when men are afraid of the light.* Your eyes will adjust to the *light* soon enough. Be not afraid. Dare to walk down the new lighted path. Abundant life is just around the bend for those who chase on...

Day 65

SPEEDING ALONG...

"A speeding fine lets me know it's OK to break the law, just so long as I'm willing pay money for the privilege to do so." —Jarod Kintz

For Christ is the end of the Law for righteousness to everyone who believes.
(Romans 10:4)

Oh the joy of discovering the death of Law as a means of righteousness before the King in the chase after the Serving King. The novice, freed from the need to obey Law in acquiring righteousness, replaced by the righteousness of the Serving King, often abandons Law entirely, delighted to discover *speeding along* now an acceptable form of *'being and doing'*, thanks to Him who has paid the fine. And indeed, the Serving King has paid the fine in full, rest assured.

But deep into the chase, the consequences of *speeding along* soon begin to overwhelm those whose fines have been paid. Eventually, the realization arrives that every moment of *speeding along* comes with consequences independent of the fine the Serving King has paid. And while obedience to the *Law of the Spirit*, just like obedience to the Law, offers no usable righteousness in the presence of the King, it does usher in the *abundant life* of which the Serving King so often speaks. Consequences matter.

So the novice soon discovers the joy of obedience to the *Spirit of the Law* and the abundant life made possible to those delighting in *'being and doing'* in the ways of the Serving King. The danger for every novice chaser is the great temptation to begin correlating abundant life with actual righteousness before the King. A tragic mistake indeed. Christ is the end of Law in every form in regards to righteousness before the King. There is no righteousness but His.

Thus, the novice finally begins to cease *speeding along,* even though the *fine* has been paid. Every novice arrives at the same conclusion. It is not simply ok to break the law. Life can never be the same for those who finally learn to stop *speeding along* as they chase on...

Day 66

SECOND FIDDLE...

"The end of law is not to abolish or restrain, but to preserve and enlarge freedom. For in all the states of created beings capable of law, where there is no law, there is no freedom." —John Locke

For Moses writes about the righteousness that is based on the law, that the person who does the commandments shall live by them.
(Romans 10:5)

Freedom, like so many other aspects of life, thrives best in a world where freedom plays second fiddle, liberated from having to be king. Left to its own devices, its own lordship, freedom runs amuck, unrestrained by its cousin and friend: law. Lacking direction, freedom runs down all available roads, many of which debilitate, impeding all future travels. Freedom longs for a companion able to point to the right roads. Once liberated from lordship, no longer forced to navigate its own path, freedom thrives in the confines of law.

Faith, the footstool of righteousness, embraces law, not as a means of righteousness before God; rather, a means by which freedom is contained, enabling its master to live safely and comfortably within the guidelines provided by law. The novice, enjoying the safety and comfort of law, will soon drift into thinking righteousness is the by-product of living within the guidelines of law. But law does not make one righteous, nor does obedience, limited as obedience may be. Law simply enlarges freedom, providing authentic freedom guidelines for exercising freedom across the broadest spectrum possible.

Thus, the second fiddle, freedom, does not ask, "Can I do this?" for indeed you can; instead, freedom asks, "Should I do this?" The latter is a very different question indeed. The latter pursues that which enhances and builds up. It ignores that which destroys and maims.

Hence, the wise among us are free to pursue that which edifies. And law, the companion to faith, points to that which edifies. You are free to pursue all roads, but freedom, genuine freedom, always seeks the path of edification. As you travel the road of freedom, ignore the pretense of righteousness; such is never the case, even on your best days. Instead, freedom 'lives by them' in pursuit of that which edifies. Such is the life of those chasing on...

Day 67

UP OR DOWN...

"Your time is limited, so don't waste it living someone else's life. Don't be trapped by dogma–which is living with the results of other people's thinking. Don't let the noise of others' opinions drown out your own inner voice. And most important, have the courage to follow your heart and intuition."
—Steve Jobs

But the righteousness based on faith says, "Do not say in your heart, 'Who will ascend into heaven?' " (that is, to bring Christ down) "or 'Who will descend into the abyss?' " (that is, to bring Christ up from the dead).
(Romans 10:6-7)

Doing, behaving well, is a difficult concept to root out as a ground for right standing before God. It lingers in the heart, continuing to ask the redundant question, "What must I do?" So Paul acknowledges the constant quest for right behavior. Should I ascend into heaven or down into the abyss? Which one would please God, make me righteous before the God? And, of course, the answer, so foreign to our way of thinking, is simply do nothing. Every *'doing'* has been tried before. And yes, they have all failed.

The righteousness of faith depends on 'doing' not at all. In its place is a simple and profound dependence upon Jesus as the only ground for salvation. There is no road to righteousness other than through Jesus Christ. He is the ground of salvation for all those who will stand before God.

The dogma of those insisting on working their way toward a right relationship with God is a dogma that must be jettisoned once and for all. Set the heart free to finally rest in Jesus, to trust Him as the only means of salvation. He is our righteousness. And the heart knows this truth to be so. It is intuitive. So comes the need to listen to your heart in its quest for the righteousness of faith. The heart knows *'works of the law'* lead to a dead-end street, a no-way out adventure, void of power and righteousness. Only faith in Him liberates the heart to radically chase after Jesus, to recklessly abandon all works, resting only in Him.

But the noise of those working hard will lure you back to the way of *'works'* righteousness. Resist the temptation. Instead, keep your eyes on Him who liberates from the need to work. And yes, once freed, genuinely freed, you will chase after His way of 'being and doing' but not as a means of righteousness; rather, because the righteousness of faith has finally taken root. Chase on...

Day 68

HOBBIT SPEAK...

"I should like to save the Shire, if I could—though there have been times when I thought the inhabitants too stupid and dull for words, and have felt that an earthquake or an invasion of dragons might be good for them."
—J. R. Tolkien

But what does it say? "The word is near you, in your mouth and in your heart" (that is, the word of faith that we proclaim).
(Romans 10:8)

Many chasing after the Serving King desire to *save the shire* between bouts of thinking *the inhabitants too stupid or dull for words.* And to be fair to *hobbits* who think poorly of the shire inhabitants, mere words rarely bring about the salvation of the shire; hence, the eventual assessment of *too stupid and dull for words.* And countless are the hours spent laboring in the realm of mere words for the sake of the *too stupid and dull.* But no hobbit can labor endlessly in the land of mere words without eventually succumbing to silence, the cessation of proclamation, the end of hope in mere words.

But the *Word* of God is no mere word, powerless and ineffectual in the mind and heart of the dull-witted. To the contrary, the *Word* is alive, powerful and effective in bringing about transformation in the dullest of wits. Thus, wise are those proclaimers who learn the art of proclaiming *Word* in the grandest forms of simplicity, casting seed recklessly across the broadest spectrum possible, knowing the intrusive power of *Word.* They have watched and listened to the power of the invasive *Word* coming from the mouth of the Serving King. More to the point, they were once in the throng of the *too stupid and dull for words,* until the meddlesome seed penetrated *mouth and heart. Word* is a powerful force of enlightenment, even for the dullest of wits.

Thus, those chasing after the Serving King soon join the chorus of proclaimers, those anxiously and readily engaged in the songs of the professed, the proclamation of *Word.* And so the seed leaves the hands of the sowers invading the lives of all those within sowing distance, infected by the invasive power of the seed. The sower's job is done for now as the seed begins its invasive burrowing into the soon no longer *too stupid and dull for words.* It is the way of the Word from those still chasing on...

Day 69

HOBBITS AGAIN...

"Courage is found in unlikely places." —J. R. R. Tolkien

Because, if you confess with your mouth that Jesus is Lord
and believe in your heart that God raised Him from the dead, you will be saved.
(Romans 10:9)

The courage to step away from the crowd is the rarest of finds. Yet, lurking in the most *unlikely places,* deep within the crevices of the human heart, the wheelhouse of the heart, is an untapped reservoir waiting to be exploited, ready to unleash salvation into the lives of those willing to step out in faith. Faith empowers those who leave the comfort of the masses. But courage must find expression, verbalization, as the *mouth confesses* the convictions brewing deep within. But the crowd, schooled in the rigors of conformity, insists on *political correctness* regarding all things flowing from the mouth. Anyone is free to *think* what they may, as long as all verbal expressions are conformed to the mood of the crowd, external conformity at all times. Political correctness at every turn.

Even entrance into the Kingdom of God is governed by the boldness to speak, a readiness to verbalize the courage brewing in the *unlikely places. So* the hobbits amongst us begin to rise up in the midst of the crowd, willing to risk the trauma of actually speaking, confessing, allegiance to the Serving King. The willingness to speak is indeed the first step of salvation.

But like all quests toward salvation, the journey for those confessing the Lordship of Jesus is often just that, a journey toward salvation. Salvation rarely comes without an arduous journey into the unknown, His way of *'being and doing'.* And like all hobbits on the quest after the Serving King, you will be tempted to trail along in silence, undetected by the watchful eye of the crowd. But silence is never His way. Only those courageous enough to confess will find the salvation offered by the King. And courage appears in the *unlikely places,* the mouth of those willing to risk the wrath of the masses toward those willing to boldly leave silence behind as they chase on...

Day 70

NO SHAME...

*"Shame is the most powerful, master emotion.
It's the fear that we're not good enough."* —Brene Brown

*For the Scripture says, "Everyone who believes in Him will not be put to shame."
(Romans 10:11)*

I t is the inevitable consequence of chasing closely after the Serving King, residing in His proximity. It arrives not because the Serving King does or says anything to remind you of your shortcomings; rather, His *'being and doing'* simply emanates a *goodness* far beyond what those following Him can accomplish. And so, the many, too uncomfortable in His presence to bear the *master emotion shame,* soon begin to drift farther and farther behind Him, allowing the distance between them to ease the sense of *shame.*

And as the Serving King walks farther and farther ahead, His ways of *'being and doing'* fades from sight, even from memory, leaving in its place the *'being and doing'* of others equally inept at *'being and doing'* in the ways of the Serving King. So the company of the substandard grows as the Serving King treks on in the distance. Then comes the temptation to rid oneself of *shame* simply by lowering the standard of *'being and doing'* to the level of the crowd, a workable standard for even the most average follower of the Serving King. Thus, the proclamation of grace rings through the masses as they celebrate His love and grace toward those so inept in His ways of *'being and doing'.* And indeed, His love abounds toward the inept, those too fearful of failure to even try.

But there is another way, His way, eliminating *shame* from the life of those chasing after the Serving King. It is the way of proximity, remaining close enough to the Serving King to hear His voice, His proclamation, "Job well done, good and faithful servant." It is the way of those understanding how far they have come in this quest after the Serving King and how far there is yet to go for those who continue on in the chase after the Serving King...

Day 71

DISTINCTION...

*"Distinctions drawn by the mind are not necessarily equivalent
to distinctions in reality." —Thomas Aquinas*

*For there is no distinction between Jew and Greek;
for the same Lord is Lord of all, bestowing His riches on all who call on Him.
(Romans 10:12)*

The *distinctions* in those chasing together after the Serving King are nearly impossible to miss. Hence, the reality of *Jew and Greek* and the seemingly endless addition of other clans, Pentecostals, Catholics, Baptists, Lutherans, Jehovah's Witness, etc. And most trekkers, unintentionally or not, drift toward those who trek in like-minded fashion. As the old saying goes, "Birds of a feather flock together." And so, the clans trek after the Serving King in cadence to the ways of *'being and doing'* most comfortable to those so engaged.

And each clan, confident in its encounter with the Serving King, secretly merely tolerates the others, those poor souls whose encounter lacks missing key ingredients made known only to the King's favorites, His beloved people, the clan so chosen by each one chasing after the Serving King. On they go in peaceful co-existence with those who simply have not seen all there is to be seen. And try as they may, the distinctions in the clans prevent any real merging of the clans; and so, the parade of the clans following the Serving King continues down the avenue, each vying for the attention of the crowd.

But the reality from the King's perspective is a very different reality than the one created *by the mind* of those chasing after the Serving King. The King sees no distinction in those who call on Him. The King cares not for the color and shape of their clothes, the theology dictating this or that behavior, nor even the confessions shaping faith and life. The King cares not if they are loud or quiet, contemplative or playful, rich or poor, nor anything else made distinctive by the clans. The only concern of the King, and, yes, it is the King's only concern in matters of salvation, is their *call on Him*. Chase on with all those who call upon the name of the Lord...

Day 72

THE BRIDGE...

"Nothing makes one feel so strong as a call for help." —Pope Paul VI

For "everyone who calls on the name of the Lord will be saved."
(Romans 10:13)

The gatherings of those chasing after the Serving King are endlessly creating distinctions for their own tribe, points of identification, each claiming to see clearly what the others have so plainly missed; but the basis for salvation, *calling on the name of the Lord,* has never changed. So Paul revisits the words of the prophet Joel, "...everyone who calls on the name of the Lord shall be saved" (Joel 2:32). *Calling on the name of the Lord* is the bridge to all who would seek to cross into the Kingdom of Heaven, *the access key,* the way into the presence of God.

Still, the tribes continue in their persistent claim to see better, to know God in a way distinct from all the others. But the *bridge* remains, undamaged by those who seek to modify it, to claim it as their very own, granting access to all who would *call on the name of the Lord.* The *bridge* has always been and always will be. The tribes, try as they may, can do nothing to limit access to any who *calls on the name of the Lord.*

Over the millenniums, the tribes chasing after the Serving King have all *named* this Lord, seeking to know God by naming God, labels of all kinds, each intended to grant easier accessibility to those seeking to *call on the name of the Lord.* Thus, there is the endless array of *names* attempting to describe what cannot be described, that which extends far beyond any attempt to label.

But understand, the Lord speaks all languages, comprehending every effort to *name* Him, to label God, providing easy access to *the bridge, calling on the name of the Lord.* And so, the promise of God remains, "And it shall come to pass afterward, that I will pour out my Spirit on all flesh..." (Joel 2:28). Therefore, they come from all nations and peoples crossing *the bridge,* empowered by the *Spirit on all flesh, calling on the name of the Lord,* as they chase on after the Serving King...

Day 73

WITNESS...

"It takes two to speak the truth: one to speak, and another to hear."
—Henry David Thoreau

How then will they call on Him in whom they have not believed?
And how are they to believe in Him of whom they have never heard?
And how are they to hear without someone preaching?
(Romans 10:14)

Novices often chase after the Serving King in silence too enthralled by His presence to do anything but follow, too absorbed in listening and learning to ever speak aloud, too intimidated by the potential consequences of speaking to ever verbalize allegiance to the Serving King. It is the process of the growing novice fully engaged in learning the art of *'being and doing'* in the ways of the Serving King. This is the first stage of being a *witness,* a learner, seeing and hearing what so many long to see and hear.

But the call to be a *witness,* "...you will be My witnesses in Jerusalem and in all Judea and Samaria, and to the end of the earth" (Acts 1:8), is never about continuing the chase in silence, nor is it a command to summon up the enthusiasm and courage to speak; rather, it is simply the by-product of receiving the *power* promised by Jesus, "But you will receive power when the Holy Spirit has come upon you" (Acts 1:8). *Speaking* is the fruit of the Spirit of God, the manifestation of His presence, the unexpected flip side of being a *witness.*

The *power* to speak of Jesus, His ways of *'being and doing'*, is the evidence of the Holy Spirit, the second stage necessary for all would be *witnesses* engaged in the chase after the Serving King. You will be tempted to regulate all *speaking* in relationship to the response of those who are *hearing* or, more to the point, to those who seem to hear so little. But the *witness* is never concerned with the *ability to hear,* that, too, a fruit of the Spirit. The *witness* merely speaks of that which has been seen and heard while chasing after the Serving King. And those who have *witnessed* much can never chase in silence again. Witnesses speak as they chase on...

Day 74

NO NEWS...

"No news is good news!" —*an idiom from days gone by*

And how are they to preach unless they are sent? As it is written,
"How beautiful are the feet of those who preach the good news!"
(Romans 10:15)

Silent chasers, novices engaged in the quest to stay on the heels of Jesus, create a world in which the *Good News* of Gospel rarely finds its way into the public square, even as those chasing after the Serving King stroll along. And those manning the public square are too often thrilled by a lack of news concerning the Serving King. So their declaration, "No news is good news!" Alas, the public square remains void of *good news*. And so, ugly feet often rule the day in the public square.

But those chasing after the Serving King soon discover an inability to remain silent even in the public square. Silence is simply not a viable option for those in whom the Spirit of God is at work, bringing about His ways of *'being and doing'*, enabling all those chasing after the Serving King to learn to speak, to share *good news*. And this is, indeed, *good news*.

However, those who learn to speak often lose the ability to walk, to engage the feet in continuing to chase after the Serving King. Instead, those learning to speak often find the public square far too dangerous a place to announce *good news* and so the retreat from the public square back to the safe confines of the sheep pen, the gathering of the like-minded. And, oh, the glorious conversation amongst those gathered in the safety of the sheep pen. Stories of *good news* reverberate amongst the like-minded, reminding them of just how *good* the *news* really is.

But the Serving King is never content to remain in the safety of sheep pen. And so, the like-minded soon discover the absence of Him who continues to return to the public square, searching for that which is lost, those whose lives are yet untouched by *good news*. The chase after the Serving King can never remain in the comfort of the sheep pen...

Day 75

STORYTELLERS...

"I'm a storyteller; that's what exploration really is all about. Going to places where others haven't been and returning to tell a story they haven't heard before." —James Cameron

But they have not all obeyed the gospel.
For Isaiah says, "Lord, who has believed what he has heard from us?"
(Romans 10:16)

Preaching, clad in beautiful feet or not, often goes unheeded, falling on ears deaf to the things of the Kingdom of God. And the novice chaser, forgetting that *others haven't been there*, is often discouraged by the lack of receptivity in those who hear the *Good News*. Tragically, *storytellers* soon stop telling stories, discouraged that others fail to engage, fail to join the chase after the Serving King.

But *storytellers* who continue to chase after the Serving King, who *have been there*, more importantly, *are there*, simply cannot resist telling tales of what the Serving King has done, is doing, in and for those chasing along behind Him. Storytelling is the fruit of having *been there*, experiencing the vitality and thrill of chasing after the Serving King.

And *storytellers* soon cease to worry about who has believed or who is obeying. The response of others is never their concern, never the motivation for the tales, never the reason for storytelling at all. Storytellers soon learn there is one who always listens, always delights in the details of every tale, always applauds at the finish of every story. Every story finds the ears of the King, and the tales of the adventures of His Son and those who follow Him never go unheard, never unappreciated.

So comes the challenge to join the exploration, to chase closely after the Serving King, and to tell the stories of those adventures. Soon will arrive the day when an audience gathers, thrilled to hear the stories as you excitedly retell the details of every adventure to Him who always hangs on every word. But you will not see the crowd gathering to hear the story. Your eyes will always be on Him who is thrilled with every adventure. Go ahead. Tell the story of your grand adventure as you chased on...

Day 76

SELECTIVE HEARING...

"I have selective hearing." —Eddie Van Halen

So faith comes from hearing, and hearing through the word of Christ.
(Romans 10:17)

S torytelling, the inevitable fruit of chasing after the Serving King, becomes a way of life. Tragically, the many, having left the heels of the Serving King long ago to remain in the safety of the sheep pen, in proximity to those inclined to tell yesterday's stories, only tell stories of adventure from a past long ago. And so, the sheep pen resonates with old stories, glorious as they are, celebrating the adventures of days gone by when the heels of the Serving King were still close at hand.

But those still engaged, close on the heels of the Serving King, rarely spend days in the sheep pen, safely tucked away from those whose *selective hearing* makes storytelling the grandest of all challenges. Outside the sheep pen, the world is full of those whose hearing is *selective,* carefully avoiding tales of the present moment, today's adventures with the Serving King. *Selective hearers* have mastered the art of distraction, skilled in the tools of avoidance, able to shield the ears from the nuisance of *storytellers*. Theirs is a world filled with noise and activity of every kind. Anything necessary to drown out the tales of today's adventures on the heels of the Serving King.

However, storytellers understand the power of the *Word of Christ* to break through the protective walls of even the most determined *selective hearers,* those skilled in the methods of evasion, *virtuosoes* in the art of *selective hearing*. There is no hiding from the *Word of Christ,* try as one may. And so, the charade of *selective hearing* crumbles in the presence of storytellers, those proclaiming the *Word of Christ* in the present moment, stories of today's adventures with the Serving King. Storytellers ramble on too excited about today's adventures to walk in silence. And the charade of *selective hearing* fades in the presence of His storytellers, filled with the excitement of chasing on...

Day 77

STORYTELLERS...

"Storytelling is the most powerful way to put ideas into the world today."
—Robert McAfee Brown

But I ask, have they not heard? Indeed they have, for
"Their voice has gone out to all the earth,
and their words to the ends of the world."
(Romans 10:18)

The twitter generation, faster than any generation before them, still tells stories. Their stories, different than earlier storytellers, deploy tools of another kind. Twitter, Instagram, Snapchat, WhatsApp, and the list goes on. Gone are the days of lore, stories far beyond the limits of 140 characters, tales stretching the imagination to its farthest limits. But make no mistake, stories have not died, they have simply evolved into tales of another kind, tales for a generation on the fly. Don't expect them to slow down, unless you have a story to tell...

The stories they yearn to hear, stories beyond the limits of 140, are stories of the grandest kind, stories stirring the heart with hope for redemption and transformation. They are not the tales from history, stories of grand adventures from eras long gone. No, the stories they love are the stories of today, the tales of the present moment, pictures of what is happening now.

The snapshots, personal and current, must be real, pictures of what God is doing in the present moment. Selfies, the modern story, must reflect reality, transformation as it is unfolding in the life of those touched by the grace of God. You will be hesitant, fearful this 'judge me not' generation will, in fact, judge you. Such is the way of those declaring acceptance of all, all but those most radically transformed by the grace of God. Nonetheless, throw off the yoke of acceptance, dare to be profoundly different, transformed by the grace of God unfolding in your life. And as the Serving King transforms the very essence of your 'being and doing', take the shot, the selfie proclaiming the picture of a thousand words, and share it across the vast spectrum of your social media world. Join the throng of those whose "..voice has gone out to all the earth." Snap the chase after the Serving King...

Day 78

JEALOUS...

"Being jealous of a beautiful woman is not going to make you more beautiful."
—Zsa Zsa Garbor

But I ask, did Israel not understand? First Moses says,
"I will make you jealous of those who are not a nation;
with a foolish nation I will make you angry."
(Romans 10:19)

Jealously haunts us all, like it or not. But, sooner or later, awareness finally appears over the horizon, enlightening you, reminding you jealously has no purpose other than to drive the most jealous to action. This is never more true than for those who were once beautiful themselves, once favored in days gone by. But, alas, beauty is always fragile, always at risk, always threatened by those daring to be more beautiful. And the beauty God desires is forever available to anyone willing to chase after the Serving King. Yes, it is always possible to be more beautiful than you are in the present moment. Faithfulness knows no limit as it expands exponentially in the heart of those chasing hardest after the Serving King.

Israel, long the favorite child, basked in the limelight, favored nation status of the highest kind. But favor can create an unintended consequence, laziness robbing the favored nation of vitality and zeal. It is the dangerous companion to favored nation status; likewise for people as well. The Serving King is relentless in His quest to transform those remaining on His heels as He climbs to the highest points, those places reflecting His ways of 'being and doing'.

Some, fatiguing of the chase, envy those who carry on, never losing sight of the Serving King as He crosses the landscape. Jealousy rising, some will simply quit, angered by those who would dare to stay on His heels as others fall behind. Others, seeing what God is doing in the lives of those staying on the heels of the Serving King, refuse to surrender, reengage, and soon discover their luster returning as never before. And then, the unexpected fruit appears for those staying in the chase. Focused on Him, all others fall from sight, jealousy gone, the radiance from Him consuming every eye. Chase on till all jealousy has died...

Day 79

OMNIPRESENT...

"How often I found where I should be going only by setting out for somewhere else." —R. Buckminster Fuller

Then Isaiah is so bold as to say,
"I have been found by those who did not seek Me;
I have shown Myself to those who did not ask for Me."
(Romans 10:20)

Many who journey, either by accident or intent, set an evasive course steering clear of God and those who trek after the Serving King. Some of the most determined create evasive tactics of all kinds, filling life with distractions great and small. Many are those consuming the mundane, meaningless this and thats, all mere diversions from that which cannot be ignored. Some fill life with evils of many kinds, thinking God hesitate to invade the presence of evil, all the anti-gods of life.

But God can never be evaded, try as one may, regardless of the trails one travels. So God's proclamation "I have been found by those who did not seek Me." Finding God is the ultimate destination for all who journey irregardless of the efforts to avoid God's presence. It is the very nature of God to be found, "I have shown Myself to those who did not ask for Me." No one can avoid that which cannot be avoided.

And with the discovery of God comes accountability before God. For only in knowing God can anyone be held accountable before God. Hence, the many hide thinking God content to ignore their ignorance, void of knowledge, safe in the glory of cluelessness. Tragically, no such condition ever exists, not ever.

But accountability is never the primary motivation for God's self-revelation. Love drives God, mandating efforts great and small, all expressions of God's profound love and concern for every dimension of His creation. So God makes God known to all who journey through life. For only in knowing God can anyone find *life*. And so, the reality for all who journey, "...I found where I should be going only be setting out for somewhere else." And yes, in the end, all journeys end at the feet of the King. Chase on till His feet you have found...

Day 80

MAN'S ORIGINAL VIRTUE...

"Disobedience, in the eyes of anyone who has read history,
is a man's original virtue." —Oscar Wilde

But of Israel He says,
"All day long I have held out My hands to a disobedient and contrary people."
(Romans 10:21)

The young and inexperienced are oft prone to optimism regarding the plight of mankind or, at the very least, the developing self. The illusion, common to many still fresh into the journey of life, fills the soul with hopefulness, confidence in the power of education and opportunity to bring about a good soul. However, sooner or later, optimistic or not, a cold, hard reality begins to tarnish the idealism of youthfulness. Eventually, *"...man's original virtue"* begins to rear its ugly head: *disobedience.*

Disobedience, even to self, "...in the eyes of anyone who has read history," is the experience creating commonality amongst all who travel this path. And the novice, yet still optimistic, carries on in the hope of the dream, the vision of finding at least one who discovers deliverance from the plague of disobedience. Surely, there will be one whose *original virtue* has been untarnished by the plague, the pestilence corrupting all it touches. But no, there is no one who escapes the scourge, this "...disobedient and contrary people." And so, the illusion dies a painful death in the heart of all who once clung to the false hope.

But the plague need not continue. There is a cure made available to all persons, any who would renounce the plague and embrace the call of the Serving King. "All day long..." He has offered the cure to any and all who would repent and abandon the false hope. There is no dissuading the King. He is faithful in offering healing to all who would take it.

And history is His-story, a tale of redemption, a cleansing and healing of *man's original virtue* now long infected by the sin of Adam. His-story is the rewriting of history, a retelling, a return to the *original virtue,* the heart after God long enslaved by sin, now redeemed in His-story. Read the story again and see what God does for all who chase on...

Day 81

THE REJECTION OF RELIGION...

"Abraham is such a fascinating figure. Three world religions—Judaism, Christianity, and Islam—all claim him as a patriarch. He was raised in a religious home. And yet he rejected religion in order to pursue a personal relationship with God." —Anne Graham Lotz

I ask, then, has God rejected His people? By no means! For I myself am an Israelite, a descendant of Abraham, a member of the tribe of Benjamin. (Romans 11:1)

Religion, humanity's attempt to get to God in all of its valiant forms, fails all who pursue it. Sadly, religion can never do more than point in God's general direction, a vagueness unhelpful to those most consumed with finding a relationship with God. Still, the many fall away in their efforts to find God, to please God, heroic in their toiling to uncover God, but lost in the wilderness of religion nonetheless. All are destined for failure in the wilderness of religion.

But for all its failures, religion reveals the heart seeking God, blind as it may be, stumbling around in the mundane overtures of religion. However, the failure of religion provides the beginning of the path toward the final pursuit of God. Only those who ultimately and finally reject the folly of well-intentioned religion discover the ultimate prize, the privilege of a *personal relationship with God,* the grand prize found only in the revelation of the Christ, the mystery of Gospel.

God never rejects *His people,* those seeking to find Him, intent on pursuing a "...personal relationship with God." God is relentless, never yielding, never pausing from making Himself known to those whose heart seek knowledge of the Creator. And there stands Abraham pointing out the dangerous way for those courageous enough to leave behind the well-intentioned religion of so many others who have sought after the presence of God.

Beware, the road away from religion is often a lonely path, an isolated trek, after the Serving King, the mystery made known, the way of the Christ. And many are those too fearful of isolation to leave the comfort of the crowd and the religion they cherish. But He is faithful to seek all who are lost, all who are His people, all those still engaged in the folly of religion. Fear not. The Good Shepherd has come and will find all of His sheep yet wandering in religion even as they chase on...

Day 82

THE UNHEARD APPEAL...

"In Scripture (they say) the church is the one worldwide fellowship of believing people whose Head is Christ. It is holy because it is consecrated to God (though it is capable nonetheless of grievous sin); it is catholic because it embraces all Christians everywhere..." —J. I. Packer

God has not rejected His people whom He foreknew. Do you not know what the Scripture says of Elijah, how he appeals to God against Israel?
(Romans 11:2)

Religion, humanity's attempt to get to God, often enrages those whose paths have led to an authentic encounter with God. So Elijah appeals in vain to God, seeking God's dismissal of those who ought to know better, those kneeling at the feet of Baal, mouths that have kissed the altar of the false God (1 Kings 19:10ff). But like so many, Elijah saw only the failure of the whole, never the individual, those remaining faithful to the King, even in the backyard of Baal, even in the midst of grievous failure. God sees more, much more. God sees the heart no man can truly see.

And Elijah is not alone in the chorus of the disenchanted, the disheartened, those fatiguing of the apparent failure of God's call upon His people. Moderns, skilled in the art of judgment, soon join him in appealing to God against His Church, fallen and broken as it may appear in the midst of a lost and dying world, riddled with broken ones, all falling short of expectation. So the common fate of all those seeking God.

But God looks deeper, much deeper, into the vestiges of the human condition. There, broken and bruised, lies the remnant of those called into life by Him who never rejects His people, even in the midst of painful failure. And so, the appeal of the discouraged falls on deaf ears unwilling to yield to the pleas of the many joining the chorus of Elijah. Theirs is an unheard prayer, a plea ignored. The remnant rises to the surface in days yet to come. So God proclaims, "Yet I will leave seven thousand in Israel, all the knees that have not bowed to Baal, and every mouth that has not kissed him" (1 Kings 19:18). And it is the challenge of God to look deeper, to see what God sees breaking over the horizon of failure. They are there, still chasing on...

Day 83

DEMOLITION MAN...

"I demolish my bridges behind me–then there is no choice but forward."
—Fridtjof Nansen

"Lord, they have killed Your prophets, they have demolished Your altars,
and I alone am left, and they seek my life."
(Romans 11:3)

Religion, humanity's attempt to discover God, litters the landscape, offering a variety of paths toward God too often claiming sovereignty over all efforts to find God. And rarely do those claiming to have found the way to God play well with others equally confident of the path to God. So the *demolition man* often appears, unleashing a path of destruction upon all alternative trails, other ways of moving toward the King. Modern chaos erupts as religions war for the hearts of humanity.

But in the midst of the carnage, there often rises a voice willing to proclaim the goodness of God, His way of *'being and doing'*, a way other than demolition, so comes the Christ. And like the prophets before Him, *they seek His life*, determined to silence anyone speaking of another way, a righteousness from God. He, too, faced the carnage of the *demolition man,* those determined to silence the prophets of God, to remove the testimony of those who have found Him.

Nonetheless, those who encounter God, genuinely encounter God, simply cannot be silent regardless of those who *"...seek my life."* Silence is simply never an option for those whom God has touched. Those chasing after the Serving King know the dangers of testifying to the grace of God, His way of *'being and doing'.* And when the *demolition man* comes your way, you will join Elijah in proclaiming, "Lord, they have killed Your prophets...and they seek my life." And in that moment, you will be tempted to become the *demolition man* mandating the destruction of all who oppose your testimony for God. But the Serving King rarely becomes the *demolition man.* Nor will He allow those who trek after Him to join the carnage of religion. His is another way, the way of grace. And it is costly for all who dare to walk in His way as they chase on...

Day 84

NEUTRALITY...

"The hottest place in Hell is reserved for those who remain neutral in times of great moral conflict." —Martin Luther King, Jr.

But what is God's reply to him? "I have kept for Myself seven thousand men who have not bowed the knee to Baal".
(Romans 11:4)

E xile, the modern state of affairs, is never pleasant for those chasing after the Serving King. Too uncomfortable to carry on, many knelt long ago to the pagan god, surrendering all things Christian to the demi-god ruling the present age. Sadly, comfort too often reigns over allegiance to the truth. Baal, the name of old, has merely evolved to nomenclature more appealing to the modern mind. Humanism, liberalism, atheism are only names for any god other than God. Kneeling, they live in peace, abandoning His ways of 'being and doing'.

Still others, perhaps, most of the others, have neither knelt nor given up the chase after the Serving King; instead, resting in a quiet neutrality, hopeful the Serving King will turn around and come back for those waiting for His return. Fearful of moral conflict with both Baal and the Serving King, theirs is an existence of neutrality, poised and ready to join the winning team should a final victor arise. Thus, the warning from Martin Luther King, Jr., "...the hottest place in hell is reserved for those who remain neutral in great moral conflict." And yes, the conflict is indeed a great moral conflict.

But every age has those faithfully chasing after the Serving King. They refuse to bow to Baal regardless of the name, ever faithful in the chase. Refusing to capitulate, they remain on His heels, determined to stay faithful regardless the cost. And their chase never goes unnoticed by Him whose eye never closes. He sees their pursuit and knows they are amongst those who have refused to bow, those "...who have not bowed the knee to Baal." Nor is He the only one watching. Baal sees their tenacity, as well, their way of "being and doing', His way of 'being and doing' alive and well in those refusing to bow. Chase on knowing eyes are upon you...

Day 85

HEROIC SIRES...

"If your descent is from heroic sires, show in your life a remnant of their fires."
—Nicolas Boileau-Despreaux

So too at the present time there is a remnant, chosen by grace.
(Romans 11:5)

Discussions of *remnant*, leftovers from a previous generation, are always the by-product of decay, painful decay, in which the *passion* of the *heroic sires* are not successfully transferred to the majority of the next generation. Thus, the old saying often heard in communities of faith, "There are no spiritual grand-children." Reality reminds us that every person must actualize their own faith, the by-product of a profound encounter with the Serving King.

But communities of faith rarely see the heritage of *heroic sires* broadly trans-late into lives following in the footsteps of those who have gone before. Instead, the devotion of the previous generation all too often fades as the lineage moves forward void of a passionate encounter with the Serving King; instead, only the patterns of chasing after the Serving King are transferred. And patterns, void of passions birthed in an authentic encounter, merely become *legalism,* bereft of much-needed passion, the fruit of an encounter with the Serving King. So his-tory's repeated tale of communities of faith whose *fires* rarely cross from gen-eration to generation.

The best any follower of the Serving King can do is to *sire* the environment in which an authentic encounter with the Serving King can actually occur. But it is only the King Himself who can ignite the passion necessary to sustain a lifelong trek, infusing dull patterns of living with vitality, enabling the remnant to carry on. So the remnant, those who have genuinely encountered the King, remains in every new generation.

And the *remnant* always evidences the *heroic sires* in their day-to-day life. It is not simply the encounter with the King but additionally, the rich heritage of the *heroic sires* providing a way of *'being and doing'* that has guided generations before. Thus, the *remnant* always rests on the proven foundation of previous chasers. Add to the foundation of the saints as you chase on...

Day 86

WORMHOLES...

"The meaning of life. The wasted years of life. The poor choices of life. God answers the mess of life with one word: grace." —Brennan Manning

But if it is by grace, it is no longer on the basis of works;
otherwise grace would no longer be grace.
(Romans 11:6)

The novice trekker, fully aware of inabilities of every kind, has no illusions of *working* one's way into the Kingdom of God. The *mess of life* is simply too overwhelming for the illusion of self-righteousness before God. No such folly peaks over the horizon until *grace,* God's unmerited forgiveness and assistance in the *mess of life,* begins its astonishing metamorphosis in those chasing after the Serving King. Transformation is the incredible, unbelievable, unanticipated, and unavoidable consequence of a bona fide encounter with *grace. Works* are simply unavoidable in a life touched by *grace.* And so, the unintended consequence appears, the emerging *wormhole* taking shape as it spins toward *grace...*

Unprepared for the dynamic transformation of *grace,* a rigorous overhaul from the inside out, the novice naively assumes God must be pleased by emerging works unfolding in the life of those chasing deeper and deeper into the quest after the Serving King. And so, God is. But naivety blinds the novice to the coming temptation to undermine the foundation of *grace* with *works* burrowing their way under God's intended foundation of *grace.* And with each passing day, each victory, each step, in the right direction, the wormhole undermines *grace* as the foundation of a relationship with the King. Soon, works, the fruit of *grace,* erodes the soil under *grace's* foundation.

But the illusion is short-lived, as the *mess of life* always reappears in every journey, quickly filling the wormhole, removing the illusion of *'being and doing'* in a manner suitable to the standards of the King. Soon enough, failure reappears and gone is the pretense of earning one's place at the table of the King. Still, the foundation of *grace* reappears, strong and sturdy, as the *mess of life* fills all wormholes undermining the *grace* of the Serving King. Chase on into the arms of grace...

Day 87

THE WRONG ROAD...

"We all want progress, but if you're on the wrong road, progress means doing an about-turn and walking back to the right road; in that case, the man who turns back soonest is the most progressive." —C. S. Lewis

What then? Israel failed to obtain what it was seeking. The elect obtained it, but the rest were hardened, as it is written, "God gave them a spirit of stupor, eyes that would not see and ears that would not hear, down to this very day."
(Romans 11:7-8)

Earnest seekers, moving farther and farther down the *wrong road,* move no closer to their desired destination even with their great determination. Unfortunately, earnest intention, even from a well-intentioned heart, does little to move seekers in the right direction when heading down the *wrong road.* So Israel, determined to find God at the end of the *wrong road,* persisted in traveling farther and farther away from the God they sought, ignoring every road sign along the way, signs God placed, each pointing to the need for a u-turn, each ignored as the well-intentioned seekers sped down the wrong roadway.

Nonetheless, God determined to use Israel in spite of the dead end road upon which they traveled, blinding them to the *light,* preventing them from seeing the blatantly obvious, the undeniable, the Serving King in all of His glory. And Israel, now hardened and blind, gained speed as the *wrong road* carried them to a destination ordained for those determined to make progress down the *wrong road.*

And so, this *wrong road* dead ends at exactly the right place, the right time, the precise moment, God intended for all those determined to persist in following the *wrong road.* Standing at the end of the road, the dead end is the cross of the Christ surrounded by all the others who frantically sought to trek after the Serving King.

In that moment, the crowning moment of all creation, all roads converge, all paths unite, all persons stumble, into the presence of the Serving King, hanging upon His cross, the centerpiece of history, the destination for all who journey through life. All journeys end here at the foot of His cross, beholding Him who remained invisible to all those who went down the *wrong road.* So now that you are here, do you see Him? If you do, time to chase on...

Day 88

TURN AROUND...

*"When a train goes through a tunnel and it gets dark, you don't throw away
the ticket and jump off. You sit still and trust the engineer."*
—Corrie Ten Boom

*And David says, "Let their table become a snare and a trap, a stumbling block
and a retribution for them; let their eyes be darkened so that they cannot see,
and bend their backs forever."*
(Romans 11:9-10)

Few enthusiastic journeyers are *engineers*. Instead, most are mere passengers, reclined and relaxed, confident the train is heading in the right direction. And once engaged, few are willing to change course in midstream, to jump off the train if need be. So, enthusiastic journeys down the wrong track are often difficult to stop, nearly impossible at times, as excitement pulses through the veins of those heading in the wrong direction, confident their intended destination is just ahead.

But God's determination to use even the most off course trains often leads to *a snare*, a *stumbling block*, eyes finally darkened so that *they cannot see*, simply cannot continue on. This is no mere tunnel, a momentary blackness with light yet up ahead. This is a trap, the end of the line, a journey destined for a lifetime of darkness. It is only in the *snare,* in the utter darkness, that a decision about the *engineer* must be made. Some, having come much too far to turn back now, will simply sit in the dark, heading nowhere fast, content to let the train follow its course to wherever it may lead in the deepening darkness. Too much invested to turn back now. These are those who *bend their backs forever,* destined to reside in darkness endlessly.

But there a few, perhaps a very few, who finally determine, "I am on the wrong train, trusting in the wrong engineer, destined for dark places if I continue to *sit still*." They are no longer content to *sit still* in the unending darkness. These are those who finally understand, "...progress means doing an about-turn and walking back to the right road; in that case, the man who turns back soonest is the most progressive" (C.S. Lewis). And so, the journey backwards begins for those no longer content to simply *sit still*. They have finally decided to chase backwards toward the Serving King...

Day 89

UNAWARES OF THE FALL...

"We stumble and fall constantly even when we are most enlightened. But when we are in true spiritual darkness, we do not even know that we have fallen."
—*Thomas Merton*

So I ask, did they stumble in order that they might fall? By no means! Rather through their trespass salvation has come to the Gentiles,
so as to make Israel jealous.
(Romans 11:11)

L ittle surprise when the blind *stumble* around in their efforts to reach every person's destination, an audience with the King, intended or not. Such is the fate for those living in darkness, blinded to the light emanating from the Serving King. But more tragic than any fall, painful as falls can be, is an ignorance of the *fall* itself. Ignorance regarding the fall *is* a cruel fate common in all those whose backs have *bent forever*. The fallen, *unawares of the fall*, soon accommodate to their fallen state, content in their fallen condition, their fallen surroundings.

So they stood proclaiming death for the Serving King, the chant of the blinded ones, unawares of their fallenness, still confident of their trek toward the King. The Serving King, knowing their blindness, embraces their call, confident in the King who uses even the *unawares* in fulfilling a destiny that cannot be avoided. So even the *fallen*, ignorant of their condition, have a place in the purpose of the King. *Their trespass,* the unavoidable consequence of all who fall, ushered in salvation for the Gentiles, completing the divine purpose for those *unawares of the fall*. And so, they departed in the same condition they arrived, fallen, blinded to the Kingdom crashing in upon all who journey, ignorant of the hand of God weaving history right before their eyes.

You, too, will have many days of ignorance, unawares you have fallen, blinded to the purposes of God unfolding before you as you go. And like those who have fallen before you, the King will seize your condition using it for His purposes as they unfold around you. Yes, even in your fallenness, the King is at work bringing about His purposes. You simply cannot fall far enough to be beyond usefulness for the King. But it's never too late to get up and chase on...

Day 90

REBELLION OF A SPECIAL KIND...

"Remembering that I'll be dead soon is the most important tool I've ever encountered to help me make the big choices in life. Because almost everything—all external expectations, all pride, all fear of embarrassment or failure—these things just fall away in the face of death, leaving only what is truly important." —Steve Jobs

Now if their trespass means riches for the world, and if their failure means riches for the Gentiles, how much more will their full inclusion mean!
(Romans 11:12)

I t is an odd thing to comprehend the pervasive hand of the King in the midst of radical rebellion and failure. God weaves even a persistent refusal to see what ought to be seen or to cooperate with an undeniable destiny into His purposes. Stranger yet is the King's ability to embrace every act of rebellion turning disobedience and *failure* into *riches for the world,* the unexpected fruit of a *special kind of rebellion.*

But this is no ordinary rebellion, no run-of-the-mill failure; instead, it's a rebellion driven by passion for the King, rooted in ignorance, a track headed down the wrong road, a failure destined for success. Good intentions often fail to provide the right path for those chasing after the Serving King, and so, the well-intended often veer off course, drifting farther and farther away form the trail of the Serving King. Worse yet, good intentions often blind the well-intentioned, rendering them incapable of finding their way home, back to the path of the Serving King.

And this *rebellion of a special kind* often finds its way into the lives of those chasing after the Serving King. It is the undesirable fruit of ignorance, the eventual plight of all seeking the ways of the Serving King in self-determined ways of *'being and doing',* deemed to be the King's way, but simply are not.

But the King is well-suited for working with *rebellion of a special kind.* This kind of rebellion has often crossed the path of the King as those seeking to serve veer blindly off course. Only later will they understand the tragedy of unintentional rebellion. And only then will they see the glory of the King, as He weaves even rebellion into the purposes of the Kingdom. And, oh, the celebration as the *rebellion of a special kind* is woven back into the purpose of God. They were chasing on all along...

Day 91

PAWN...

"When you label so much of what happens to you as 'bad,' it reinforces the feeling that you are a powerless pawn at the mercy of outside forces over which you have no control. And–this is key–labeling something a bad thing almost guarantees that you'll experience it as such." —Srikumar Rao

Now I am speaking to you Gentiles. Inasmuch then as I am an apostle to the Gentiles, I magnify my ministry. (Romans 11:13)

First loves often retain a special place in the heart long after lovers have moved on. So it is in the Kingdom of God. Israel, God's first love, foolishly gave up the chase thinking His way of 'being and doing' too outlandish, too extreme, too gracious, for those chasing after God. Foolishly ignoring His pleas to remain in the chase, they, too, bowed the knee to Baal, surrendering the chase after Him.

And the new lover, intoxicated by His overture, cannot fathom a love so profound, a love deeper, older, and richer than the cross, the Son surrendered, sacrificed for 'their sake'. But God's first love remains, the focus of God's attention, a lover God still intends to redeem.

The Gentiles, too often not recognizing their role in the dance of lovers lost, fancies themselves the sparkle in God's eye, but they were not the first. The Gentiles, God's second love, are pawns in this lover's waltz, mere instruments in the effort to restore the first love.

There are indeed "...forces over which you have no control," love so profound it must redeem, must restore the luster of lovers lost. Resist the temptation to label this a bad thing. It is not. It is the same love that surrendered the Son for you as well. It is the movement of a lover whose depth and breadth of love knows no limits, no restraints, no limitations. And the same love which drives God to such extremes for the sake of God's first love is the same love which drives God to pursue you, those who have responded in faith. Like God's pursuit of Israel, so God's pursuit of you in the days yet ahead. God is relentless, loving you with such intensity, even the sacrifice of His Son is a price God is willing to pay. Chase on as God chases you...

Day 92

PROSPERITY OF RELATIONSHIP...

"Man is by nature competitive, combative, ambitious, jealous,
envious, and vengeful." —Arthur Keith

...in order somehow to make my fellow Jews jealous,
and thus save some of them.
(Romans 11:14)

Well-intentioned or not, God rarely blesses the efforts of those drifting farther and farther off the path of the Serving King. Seldom do the well-intentioned recognize the drift taking them far off course. And without intervention
of some kind, generations often wander endlessly across the barren desert, void
of the blessing of God, a relational emptiness, a wasteland. But God has a way
of wakening the spirit of nomads now in lands far from the blessing of God. God
often chases after those lost along the way.

Conversely, those chasing after the Serving King, even latecomers to the trek,
often receive the blessing God provides for those hot on the heels of Jesus. And
with that blessing comes *prosperity of relationship* with God, a keen sense of
God's presence and direction, a peace that passes all understanding, a life filled
with meaning and purpose. God's presence radiates in the community of those
chasing closely after Jesus.

Soon, those wandering in the barren desert sense the presence of God with
others, sheep of another clan enjoying the proximity of the Good Shepherd.
And so, the nature of man is quickened, calling forth the green beast, a sleeping
monster, a raging jealously, as another clan revels in the *prosperity of relationship* with God. Awakened from their slumber, jealously drives the fully awake
back into a quest after God.

Quickened by the beast, a jealously longing for a *prosperity of relationship*
now long gone, some abandon the desert wanderings, leaving behind yesterday's courtship, longing for a return to the life's first love. Fortunately, it is never
too late to run toward God, to sense His embrace, to be welcomed home into
a *prosperity of relationship*. Be prepared, there will be many newcomers to the
family of God, many unfamiliar faces, many new ways of *'being and doing'* in the
presence of the King. Together chase on...

Day 93

SHARING THE ABUNDANCE...

"Franklin Roosevelt said the test of our progress is not whether we add more to the abundance to those who have much; it is whether we provide enough to those who have too little." —Patrick J. Kennedy

For if their rejection means the reconciliation of the world, what will their acceptance mean but life from the dead?
(Romans 11:15)

Abundance liberates in ways poverty never can; never more so than with those who have entered into eternal life. Theirs is a profound understanding of endless abundance in all things. Yes, all things. And with that awareness, generosity is unleashed in ways never before imaginable. Gone are the days of worry, concern over shortages of any kind. Abundance liberates the soul.

So those chasing after the Serving King delight in His return toward the chosen people, those whom He first loved, those left behind for the moment as the Serving King called those lost in the outer realms. The Gentiles, forgotten in moments gone by, have garnered the attention of the Serving King, but only for the moment. Soon, He will return for His first love, those lingering in death, those who have lost sight of His trail. They, too, long for His return, knowing vitality is missing, lost somewhere along the quest to follow God.

But the Gentiles have learned the secret of abundance, the wellspring of all things needed for a zealous life. They have discerned His attention abounds to all who hear His voice. Every tiny voice seemingly lost in the crescendo of the mob catches His ear. No cry is lost to Him. His attention never wanes for all who call upon His name.

The Gentile, now understanding some are missing, delights in the return of the Serving King toward His first love. There is more than enough love to go around. This is an abundance of a new kind, an endless stream of all that is needed to provide vibrant life for all. And so, the celebration begins as His first love returns to the fold embraced by those whose entrance was only possible, because the first love rejected His overtures. They have awoken, seen the Serving King, returned to chasing earnestly after Him. The dead are joining the chase...

Day 94

BEYOND THE DEAD BRANCH...

"If you look closely at a tree you'll notice it's knots and dead branches, just like our bodies. What we learn is that beauty and imperfection go together wonderfully." —Matthew Fox

If the dough offered as first fruits is holy, so is the whole lump, and if the root is holy, so are the branches.
(Romans 11:16)

A close examination of the clan chasing after the Serving King always, yes always, reveals *knots and dead branches*. Hence, the beauty of the Church is never in its individual members, broken and wounded, each and everyone. To the contrary, the beauty of the Church can only be found in the whole, a comprehensive view, embracing each and every individual piece in a collective whole, *knot and dead branches* included. Only in the meshing of the collective parts does the beauty of the Church rise to the service.

The novice trekker, yet inexperienced in the beauty of the whole, the tree, often is distracted by the *dead branch*, the ugly still clinging to the tree of life. So the charge against God's Church as *dead branches* linger longer than expected. And no branch is more distracting than the branch connected to one's own tree. You will be tempted to see the *dead branch* and declare the tree deficient, unable to produce life and vitality for every part of the tree.

But not every branch will survive as the holiness of God begins to take root in trees long left without the revitalizing power of God. Some branches will simply die, falling to the wayside as the holiness of God flows into the each and every aspect of the tree. And those chasing after the Serving King begin to recognize the death of branches no longer suited for life in the holiness of God. But with each dying branch comes a new branch rising out of the holiness of God, reflecting new ways of *'being and doing'*, bringing life and vitality to trees long considered destined for the fire. Be patient as the holy root infuses life into tired limbs. And be not surprised at the magnificent beauty rising forth out of the *knots and dead branches*. Such is the incredible beauty of grace for those who chase on...

Day 95

WILD OLIVE BRANCHES...

"The demand to be loved is the greatest of all arrogant presumptions."
—Friedrich Nietzsche

*But if some of the branches were broken off, and you, although a wild olive
shoot, were grafted in among the others and now share in the nourishing
root of the olive tree, do not be arrogant toward the branches. If you are,
remember it is not you who support the root, but the root that supports you.*
(Romans 11:17)

Moderns, filled with the latest and greatest knowledge the world has to offer, often scoff at the naiveté of those who have gone before, *broken branches*, wounded by years of life in a equally broken world. It is the plague of arrogance, the fruit of wisdom harvested from the toiling of branches long gone, infecting those filled with wisdom earlier trekkers simply could not access. And with arrogance comes a sense of superiority blinding newcomers to the wealth of knowledge and wisdom established by the spreading *root* across the ages. So enters the *wild olive branches*, newcomers to the trek after the Serving King, void of history, ignorant of lessons learned by *wild olive branches* of yesteryear. History waits patiently to repeat its tale, ready to teach another generation of *wild olive branches* too arrogant to learn from those who have gone before.

Thus, modern trekkers, the latest crop of *wild olive branches*, often skip over the journeys of those who traversed the path of the King in generations passed. And so, the pages telling the stories of earlier trekkers rarely see the light of day, banished under the label *Old Testament*, deemed irrelevant by the newest *wild olives* joining the trek after the Serving King.

But sooner or later, every *wild olive branch, arrogant and abrasive,* finds its way into the grind, the grueling wheels of life, crushing all newcomers, wounding *branches*, humbling even the *wildest olive shoots*. Life spares no *wild olive branch* from the school of hard knocks. Thus, the tragedy of arrogance repeats with each new *wild olive branch*, the wheel of history cycling over and over again. However, the few, perhaps a very few, dust off the pages telling the stories of the *root*. They understand the folly of chasing after the Serving King without the wisdom of the *root*...

Day 96

ROOTS...

"Giant oak trees... have deep root systems that can extend two-and-one-half times their height. Such trees rarely are blown down regardless of how violent the storms may be." —Joseph B. Wirthlin

...do not be arrogant toward the branches. If you are, remember it is not you who support the root, but the root that supports you.
(Romans 11:18)

Those most intense in the chase after the Serving King often forget the trail has been well worn by those who chased earlier, those whose faithfulness laid the trail for others to follow. Comfortable in the well-worn trail, new chasers lose sight of the work done in days gone by, overly confident in their ability to easily find the trail. Oozing with vibrato, confident they will never abandon the trail, arrogance slowly infiltrates the heart and mind of those most zealous in the chase after the Serving King.

But many are those who once chased after the Serving King only to lose the trail as the challenges increased, the grade steepening. They, too, thought it impossible to lose His trail, to fall behind His steady pace, to lose sight of the Serving King as He quickened His gate. But failure is never wasted in the Kingdom of God. Each failure lays a stone for future followers, roots spread across the landscape, a foundation upon which all future chasers might trod. Their failures are the firm footing upon which all chasers might trek in the tumultuous days ahead.

The seasoned trekker understands the foundation built by the failures of others. They understand there is no room for arrogance in the chase after the Serving King. He darts unexpectedly this way and that, changing course at the most unexpected times, leading would-be chasers down trails yet explored. And with each new trail comes new challenges, new ways of *'being and doing'*, each more difficult than the last. He is relentless in His challenge to learn to climb even this trail, each more difficult than the trail before. Arrogance is never an option, for each one knows the precarious nature of staying on the trail of the Serving King. This is a quest only the humble dare accept as they chase after the Serving King...

Day 97

UNBELIEF...

"No man is excluded from calling upon God, the gate of salvation is set open unto all men: neither is there any other thing which keepeth us back from entering in, save only our own unbelief." —John Clavin

That is true. They were broken off because of their unbelief, but you stand fast through faith. So do not become proud, but fear. For if God did not spare the natural branches, neither will He spare you.
(Romans 11:20-21)

Early in the trek after the Serving King, *belief* flows easily and quickly, the beginner's quest always filled with baby steps, manageable for even the weakest *faith*. *Unbelief*, the inability to embrace God's revelation, never raises its head, never threatening the quest, never ushering in the possibility of *broken off*. So the novice strolls through the early days of the trek after the Serving King, *pride* rising with every step of success, the inevitable fruit of victory. Pride thrives in the early days of the quest.

But baby steps soon fade in the distance as the Serving King lengthens His stride, climbing steeper terrains, challenging the *belief* of the novice, revelation revealing increasing difficulties for those still on the trail of the Serving King. *Belief*, once easy, an effortless affair, now teeters with each new insight into His ways of *'being and doing'*.

And He will not *spare* the grafted ones, just as He did not spare the *natural branches, from* ever-increasing insights into His ways of *'being and doing'*. Each day brings new and deeper understanding into the ways of the Serving King. Prides quickly fades in the face of ever-expanding challenges along the steeping grade.

But the quest after the Serving King is never about success in *doing;* instead, it is unmitigated faith in Him who challenges, *belief* in what He can do in and through those who simply *believe*. There is nothing "...keepeth us back" but *unbelief*. So comes the challenge to step where He steps, to be and do as He does with each passing day, to understand all failures in *doing* are part of the success of *belief*. Only those too fearful to *try* will fail in the quest after the Serving King. No one is *broken off* for failure. Only *unbelief* threatens the chase after the Serving King...

Day 98

PRAGMATIC SEVERITY...

"Severity is allowable where gentleness has no effect." —Pierre Corneille

Note then the kindness and the severity of God: severity toward those who have fallen, but God's kindness to you, provided you continue in His kindness. Otherwise you too will be cut off.
(Romans 11:22)

P*ragmatic* rarely enters the conversation attempting to describe the character of God; nonetheless, God is consistently *pragmatic*, adjusting the unfolding course of history with every twist and turn in humanity's reckless journey. And the *pragmatic severity* of God is never more evident than in the cross of the Serving King, the ultimate and final pragmatic solution to the human condition. So the Serving King fleshes out the pragmatic severity of God in the harsh conditions of creation.

And those who trek after the Serving King soon learn of His *pragmatic severity* toward anyone engaged in the quest to discover His way of *'being and doing'*, the story of redemption. The seriousness of God's redemptive movement toward creation unleashes God's *pragmatic severity* in ways shocking and unexpected by those chasing after the Serving King, standing at the foot of cross, forced to embrace the pragmatism of the cross, stark and cruel beyond words. Thus, the pattern is set, a willingness to pay prices extreme, even the cruel death of the Son, all for the sake of redeeming the fallen creation.

So it causes no pause in those having witnessed the severity of the cross, as God *cuts off* anyone no longer able to aid in the redemptive movement toward the creation, His way of *'being and doing'*. The unfolding of redemption cannot be thwarted by the frailty of those unwilling or unable to *continue in His kindness.* God does not hesitate to bring in the reserves, those called to replace the *cut off* ones. And with each new generation comes a new wave of those radically determined to join Him in fleshing out the *pragmatic severity* of God, as creation is redeemed through the toil of those courageous few who continue in the *kindness of God.* For indeed, "Severity is allowable where gentleness has no effect..." Chase on into the pragmatism of God...

Day 99

PRAGMATIC RESTORATION...

*"Pragmatism asks its usual question. 'Grant an idea or belief to be true,'
it says, 'what concrete difference will its being true make
in anyone's actual life?'" —William James*

*And even they, if they do not continue in their unbelief, will be grafted in,
for God has the power to graft them in again.
(Romans 11:23)*

In the end, when all fussing and shouting is over, the pragmatism of God guides the redemptive process as it moves toward the fallen creation. Hence, *pragmatic restoration* is always, yes always, available to anyone previously *cut off* from the redemptive activity of God toward the fallen creation. *Cut-offness* is never intended to be a final state, rather a pragmatic intervention restoring vitality to the collective redemptive effort through the infusion of *new blood* as vacated roles are filled by those whose *belief* radiates life and passion.

Nor is cut-offness intended as mere punishment, banishment as a means of inflicting pain on those too timid to continue in belief; instead, cut-offness is a wake-up call, a challenge to reengage belief. It is the pragmatic means by which God reminds the cut-off ones of their intended role within God's redemptive movement toward the broken creation. It is *pragmatic alienation* offering restoration to those suddenly banished from the redemptive efforts of the Serving King.

Thus, life on the *outside* is never comfortable for those who have previously journeyed closely with the Serving King. Gone is the warmth of relationship found only in proximity to God's people, more importantly, in proximity to God Himself. In its place a hollowness develops, urging the *cut-off ones* to return to their first love, to embrace again the *belief* which once made life worth living, worth enduring, even in the most trying circumstances.

Even those who are *cut off* stand at the foot of *grace,* as the invitation to restoration stands ready to embrace any who seek a return to the redemptive effort of God. God's *pragmatic restoration* is always at work toward those who are lost to the chase...

Day 100

MOTHER NATURE...

"He not only washes him from his sins in His own blood, but He also separates him from his natural love of sin and the world, puts a new principle in his heart and makes him practically godly in life." —J.C. Ryle

For if you were cut from what is by nature a wild olive tree, and grafted, contrary to nature, into a cultivated olive tree, how much more will these, the natural branches, be grafted back into their own olive tree.
(Romans 11:24)

Moderns love the idea of the benevolence of *nature,* and what better way to express a profound confidence in *nature* than to bestow upon it the quintessential label, *mother nature,* as if *nature* embraced its inhabitants with the loving care of mother. But sooner, rather than later, all those journeying on this spinning ball discover the harsh realities of *mother nature,* fallen as she is, broken and chaotic, crippled in her feeble efforts to bask her inhabitants in *mother's love.* And so, the *natural person* begins life with *mother nature's infection,* a *natural* way of life, self-absorbed, survival of the fittest, *mother nature's* way of *'being and doing'.*

But God is never content with *wild olive trees* nurtured in the womb of *mother nature,* wild in every sense of the word. To the contrary, no one can trek after the Serving King until being *grafted* into the *cultivated olive tree,* freed from the instincts of *mother nature,* regenerated by the life-giving nutrients in the sap of a new way of *'being and doing'.*

Once grafted, *mother nature's* way of *'being and doing'* is radically altered, releasing the child of the King from being *natural,* no longer *mother nature's child,* no longer a slave to sin, no longer wild. Gone is the *"...natural love of sin and the world."* And once grafted, there is no going back even for the *cut-off ones.*

Life can never be the same once *grafted* into the *cultivated olive tree.* Once altered, *being* can never truly be *wild* again. Even the *cut-off ones* soon realize a walk on the *wild side* never truly satisfies those who have tasted the sap of the *cultivated olive tree.* And so, the *cultivated olive tree* waits patiently for the *cut-off ones* to return home to the nourishment of its life-giving sap. The chase continues...

Day 101

UNSEEN...

*"The possession of knowledge does not kill the sense of wonder
and mystery. There is always more mystery." —Anaís Nin*

*Lest you be wise in your own sight, I do not want you to be unaware of
this mystery, brothers: a partial hardening has come upon Israel,
until the fullness of the Gentiles has come in.*
(Romans 11:25)

S ome things in life are just too big, too startling, too magnificent, too revela-
tory to miss, to not comprehend. The arrival of the Serving King, the Christ,
is one of those events, undeniable at every level to those whose eyes are yet
clear, able to see. Hence, the necessity of the *unseen* in some seeking earnestly
after God. The *partial hardening* ushers in the *unseen* in the midst of the blatantly obvious, the undeniable, the impossible to miss. This *partial hardening*
blinds the eyes of those who would otherwise see. And so, the pragmatism of
God appears yet again as redemption unfolds.

And this *partial hardening* is not discipline, retribution for unfaithfulness
in days gone by; to the contrary, it is the means by which the manifestation of
the Christ must find expression. Only through the cross can the *fullness of the
Gentiles* become reality. So God ensures the cross, the centerpiece of all history,
simply by a *partial hardening* blinding decision-makers to the arrival of the Christ.
Their blindness is the key to redemption for all humanity.

Those chasing after the Serving King will often wonder, "How did I miss the
trail for so long? How did I not see what is so clear to me in this moment? Why
do I keep discovering new pieces of mystery this far down the trail?" It is the way
of *partial hardening*, the means by which the purposes of God unfold in precisely
the right manner, unquestionably the right time, in exactly the right persons.

Be of good cheer when others see so clearly what you cannot seem to grasp.
There is always purpose in the *unseen* ushering in the exactitude of the King. Rest
assured, the *unseen* is not forever; instead, only *until the fullness of the Gentiles
has come in*. Understand, *"There is always more mystery..."* in the glorious chase
after the Serving King...

Day 102

BANISHED...

"A designer knows he has achieved perfection not when there is nothing left to add, but when there is nothing left to take away."
—Antoine de Saint-Exupery

And in this way all Israel will be saved, as it is written, "The Deliverer will come from Zion, He will banish ungodliness from Jacob"; "and this will be My covenant with them when I take away their sins."
(Romans 11:26-27)

S adly, the Designer is clearly not done, for there is still so much more to be taken away from the life of those chasing after the Serving King. So the old saying, "Be patient with me, God isn't finished yet." But the *Deliverer* has come and indeed the process of *banished* has commenced in the life of all who trek after the Serving King.

Early in the process, the *Deliverer* is kind and gentle, taking only those sins willingly released, surrendered into the *banished, sins* undesirable, no longer wanted, joyfully relinquished. And so, the *Deliverer* collects the undesirable sins, removing them with each passing day, taking *away their sins* just as He promised.

Soon, the undesirables vanish into the land of *banished* never seen again, gone to places unknown. But every trekker has a dark secret known only to a trusted few, locked deep within the essence of *'being and doing'*. Hidden are the cherished *sins*, desirable, coveted deep into the trek after the Serving King. The *Deliverer* cannot be fooled, even by the most persuasive antics of those too ashamed to admit the darkest of secrets, the hidden *sins* of the flesh, too cherished to release to the *banished*. He will do no more than offer redemption, removal of the beloved hidden *sin* still eating its way into the *'being and doing'* of those most serious about chasing deeper into His way of *'being and doing'*.

Some, with trembling hands, will offer the *Deliverer* the last beloved vestiges of *sin,* mourning the loss of old ways of *'being and doing'* as the *banished* consumes them, never to be seen again. But others, unable to imagine life without old ways of *'being and doing'*, cling to them, unwilling to surrender them to the *banished* of the *Deliverer.* And so, He waits as you chase on...

Day 103

UNEXPECTED PARTNERS...

"A wise man gets more use from his enemies than a fool from his friends."
—Baltasar Gracián

As regards the gospel, they are enemies for your sake. But as regards election, they are beloved for the sake of their forefathers.
(Romans 11:28)

God never hesitates to call upon the *enemies* of a people to prepare them for redemption and restoration. More startling, perhaps, is the realization God does not hesitate to *create an enemy* for the sake of those whose destiny cannot be reshaped without the persistence of an *enemy* of great worth. And so, Israel became an *enemy* of the Gospel for the sake of those soon to be chasing after the crucified King. The trek after the Serving King is filled with *enemies,* each divinely appointed, each fulfilling destinies often unseen and incomprehensible. But, in the end, each enemy plays a vital role in the journey of those being shaped by the sovereign hand of the King.

Be leery of fatiguing of the *enemies* in life, for they are the *unexpected partners, enemies for your sake,* co-journeyers linked together in a pattern carefully woven by the King. The *wise man,* recognizing divine purpose in every enemy, *"...gets more use from his enemies than a fool from his friends."* So those chasing after the Serving King must pause long enough to examine not the enemy, but self, understanding every enemy has purpose in life. Enemies are often God-given tools of redemption and transformation.

The *fool,* confident of self-righteousness, right standing before God, spends no time with self-examination; instead, the fool stays focused on the unrighteousness of the enemy. But discovery of the enemy's unrighteousness does nothing to invalidate their purpose in the pattern of the King. God often uses the unrighteousness enemy to bring about divine purposes in the life of God's children.

Thus, the discovery of the Serving King's command to love your *enemies.* They, too, are engaged in the purposes of God. Life will be filled with *unexpected partners.* Embrace the purpose of the *unexpected partner.* Expect the unexpected as you chase on...

Day 104

GO HOME...

"No man is excluded from calling upon God, the gate of salvation is set open unto all men: neither is there any other thing which keeps us back from entering in, save only our own unbelief." —John Calvin

For the gifts and the calling of God are irrevocable.
(Romans 11:29)

T he call of God, the open invitation to come home, has never changed, always echoing across the ages, touching every heart, repeatedly, relentlessly pursuing all who have lost their way. None are spared hearing the invitation to *go home*. And the way back home is always available, always. Hence, there is no unpardonable act, only an unpardonable *state of being*, a refusal to heed the call. The remedy of that condition is always available to any willing to finally heed the call of the King.

But guilt is a terrible thing, especially in the life of one who is authentically guilty. And there is no greater sense of guilt than in the life of those already *graced*, already forgiven, but, most importantly, already enabled to live differently. Guilt like this often hinders the return home, as shame entangles the feet of those who still hear the call.

Still, the *gifts and the calling of God* are always active, always inviting even the most grievous sinner to *go home,* even those *enemies of the cross.* So those *enemies of the cross,* guilty of crucifying the Serving King, hear the ever-present song of the King inviting even the most heinous sinner to *go home.*

Nonetheless, this kind of guilt produces a debilitating unbelief, an inability to accept the reality of forgiveness for even crimes like these. Thus, the gate of salvation goes unused by those most needing restoration, forgiveness of the highest kind. Still, the song of the King continues, beckoning all who would come, to return home, to find redemption, forgiveness. The trek after the Serving King is filled with countless failures, but His call remains, the open invitation to return to the trail, to *come home.* Abandon the shame that so easily entangles. Chase Him all the way home...

Day 105

THE SWEETEST BADGE...

"Sweet Mercy is nobility's sweet badge."—William Shakespeare

For just as you were at one time disobedient to God but now have received mercy because of their disobedience...
(Romans 11:30)

Disobedience unites us all. It is the grand equalizer, the unifier for all those chasing after the Serving King. Some, long in the chase, seem to forget the failures of the past, and for good reason. Failure often brings painful memories. But failures also serve to remind us of grace, not toward others, but toward ourselves, those deep into the chase after the Serving King. Failure reminds us that things have not always been this way. Chasers, too, have a past in need of forgiveness.

But failure is not just a thing of the past; instead, it follows with us as new trails appear in the horizon. For those mature, long in the chase after the Serving King, failure in the things of old has indeed begun to wane. Maturity empowers for obedience in regards to yesterday's failures. But alas, the Serving King continues to raise the bar, to challenge those closest on His heals, to pick up the pace and join Him on even steeper trails.

It is the quest along trails yet untrod that reminds the mature of the necessity of grace, even for those most advanced in the quest. Yet ahead are failures of another kind, failures not from lack of effort but from lack of ability. Yes, He challenges even the most advanced chaser to rise to a new level, a new height requiring skills yet undeveloped, abilities still just out of reach.

It is in the failures of the present moment that God-chasers remember the joy of mercy in the past, present, and future. Mercy becomes the sweetest badge for those who are forgiven much. Gone is any pretense of pride and self-righteousness. Mercy toward self and others reigns supreme. Mercy is the badge of honor for all those still failing in the chase after the Serving King. Chase on, mercy waits...

Day 106

THE COST OF MERCY...

"I have always found that mercy bears richer fruits than strict justice."
—Abraham Lincoln

*...so they too have now been disobedient in order that by the
mercy shown to you they also may now receive mercy.
(Romans 11:31)*

M ercy is always expensive and never more than on the cross of the Serving King. The cross announces God's decision for *mercy* to reign over justice, regardless of the extreme cost to the Serving King. Justice demands an *eye for eye and a tooth for a tooth*, but *mercy* knows no such correlation. So the cross is never primarily about justice, as if justice would allow a substitute, an alternative payee; instead, it is the proclamation of *mercy* toward any and all who would accept the offer paid for by the cross of Serving King. Such is the cost of mercy. Justice howls at the inappropriateness of the innocent dying for the guilty. *Mercy* proclaims costly forgiveness for any who would embrace the ways of the Serving King. Mercy trumps justice.

And *mercy* extends a power far more productive than *justice,* bearing *"... richer fruits than strict justice."* It is the pragmatism of the King manifesting itself yet again, as the power of mercy ushers in redemption for all who would respond to the offer of the mercy, forgiveness for even the most heinous crimes.

Those who trek after the Serving King will soon discover the cost of *mercy,* as He challenges even the feeblest follower to surrender justice to the foot of the cross, the throne of mercy. You, too must heed His call to *"...pick your cross and follow Me"* (Matthew 16:24). Dare to offer mercy to those who have wronged you.

Understand, the surrendering of justice is never easy for those who have trusted justice, used it as a foundation for life, a dependable friend in hard times. But the *fruit of mercy* is a far sweeter fruit than justice can ever provide. But the *cost of mercy* is always extreme. Few are willing and able to pay it. So justice waits, knowing the many will soon return, unable to afford the cost of *mercy* in the chase after the Serving King...

Day 107

THE SHIELD OF MERCY...

*"Because it strikes me there is something greater than judgment.
I think it is called mercy." —Sebastian Barry*

*For God has consigned all to disobedience, that He may have mercy on all.
(Romans 11:32)*

The disobedience of *all* creates a lust for *justice*, or so we imagine, right until the moment *justice* comes hunting for us. And in the end, *justice* comes hunting for us all, relentless in its pursuit, for all have been *consigned to disobedience.* Only in that moment does the power of *mercy* rise to the surface ready to defend any who would hide under the *shield of mercy* arrayed on the arm of the Serving King.

Sadly, once behind the *shield of mercy*, some think God selective, offering mercy only to the *elect*, a special few, God's favorites, a cherished clan, picked from the terror of *justice* raining down on all who have been *consigned to disobedience.* But the Serving King stands beside all who journey through life, offering the *shield of mercy* to each and every one. So His Word declares, "...that He may have mercy on all."

However, the *shield of mercy* is only an invitation extended to all, each *graced,* enabled to respond in faith to the call to come under the protection of the shield, to rest in the wings of the eagle. And many have come, overjoyed to discover *something greater than judgment.* But many, too long accustomed to the ways of *justice*, refuse to hide under the *shield of mercy*; instead, they are confident to let justice reign as it pours down from heaven.

Rest assured, no one outside the shadow of the *shield of mercy* will fare well, as *justice* rains down upon those whom *justice* has courted. *Justice* spares no one. *Justice* has no friends, no favorites, no favors to offer. *Justice* is blind, slaying all who fall short of its demands. Only in the *shield of mercy* can *something greater* be found. Go ahead, come out of the rain, crawl under the *shield of mercy* as you chase on...

Day 108

GET OUT OF THE SHALLOWS...

*"Whatever you do in life, surround yourself with smart people
who'll argue with you." —John Wooden*

*Oh, the depth of the riches and wisdom and knowledge of God!
How unsearchable are His judgments and how inscrutable His ways!
(Romans 11:33)*

F ew take seriously *"...the depth of the riches and wisdom and knowledge of God."* Instead, most feast in the shallows, never considering the extent of the knowledge of God awaiting those courageous enough to dive deeply into the depth of the Word of God. The many fatten themselves on pat answers provided to those feasting in the shallows. And once fattened, few dare trek into the depths of God's Word, content to repeat the lessons of yesterday, the milk, over and over again. But sooner or later, the stories of the *shallows* begin to bore and then the exodus from the *shallows* begins as the many retreat from the water.

But some remain, sensing deeper waters just over there, right below the debating crowd, those daring to *"...surround yourself with smart people who will argue with you."* The historians in the crowd welcome the newcomers, reminding them no one has ever *touched bottom* in the quest to explore the *depth of His riches and wisdom*. But the newcomers, confident from time in the shallows, dive deeply, optimistic the *depth of His riches* lay just below.

They, too, soon discover the bottom cannot be found by those courageous enough to dive deeply, more deeply than they have ever imagined. And with each dive deeper into His Word, the pat answers float to the surface, unable to travel with those diving into the depth of His knowledge. But with each dive come new insights into the *depth of the riches*. So they return to the *shallows*, anxious to join the debate, armed with recent insights, new ways of thinking, fresh understandings.

And when boredom returns, dive deeper. Risk seeing what you have not seen before. And surround yourself with *smart people who'll argue with you.* You will also soon long for deeper dives into the depth of His Word as you chase on...

Day 109

GET STARTED...

*"If all difficulties were known at the outset of a long journey,
most of us would never start out at all." —Dan Rather*

*"For who has known the mind of the Lord, or who has been His counselor?
Or who has given a gift to Him that he might be repaid?"
(Romans 11:34-35)*

The trek after the Serving King is always a quest into the unknown. Hence, all who trek after Him do so by stepping into the darkness, the uncertainty of the path ahead, a destination unclear. Nonetheless, the early days of the trek are typically lovely walks through the garden, strolls along the river, peaceful paths in the cool shade of a brisk morning. But the trek after the Serving King is a *long journey*, spanning a lifetime, a seemingly endless array of days on end, each a bit more challenging than the one before. And with each passing day, the gardens of yesterday fade into the distance...

So arrive the *unknown difficulties* of the journey begun so very long ago, yesterday. In the moment of their arrival, these *unknown difficulties*, temptation clamors to challenge the wisdom of the Serving King, to offer Him counsel, steering away from paths steep and difficult. But distraction never dissuades the Serving King from the intended course, the journey laid out for you in days long gone, days before the foundations of the earth were set. This is the best path for you, and He cannot be persuaded to lead elsewhere, away from the path the Father has set.

Nor is there any *gift* by which the *mind of the Lord* can be averted from the destiny laid out long ago. He cannot be bribed with pleas of obedience on paths meant for another. No gift can distract His passion for obedience to the Father's destiny.

Gone is the innocence of a *long journey* unawares of the *difficulties* yet ahead. Too many difficult days have passed for innocence to remain. And so the daily challenge to *get started* on today's journey. The long journey yet ahead begins with a single step into today's unknown. Time to chase on...

Day 110

FOUNDATIONS...

"You cannot build a dream on a foundation of sand. To weather the test of storms, it must be cemented in the heart with uncompromising conviction."
—T. F. Hodge

For from Him and through Him and to Him are all things.
To Him be glory forever. Amen.
(Romans 11:36)

T he trek after the Serving King rarely sails clear of impending storms. Novice trekkers, unfamiliar with His ownership of *all things*, carry on in the midst of the ranging storm, thinking Him able to assist in overcoming the intensifying storm rising up from places unknown. And so, He can. So goes the trek in the early days of the quest.

But, eventually, the source of *all things* becomes clear as *from Him* begins to formulate in the comprehension of those paying careful attention to His mastery over *all things*. As the early disciples cower in fear with the recognition, "Who then is this, that He commands even winds and water, and they obey Him" (Luke 8:25). It is a stunning revelation, unleashing afteraffects, tremors, stressing the foundation of every trek after the Serving King.

Those surviving the shocking revelation, "...for from Him and through Him and to Him are all things," do so because the *heart* embraces an *uncompromising conviction* concerning Him. The Serving King can be trusted even in the midst of the fiercest storm, the most pressing trial, the most crushing life circumstances.

And no *foundation* can survive the raging storm without the *cement* of *absolute trust* in Him from whom all things rise. And the *glory* to Him is not the storm, impressive as it may be; rather, it is the unbroken *foundation* of all those who have cemented their quest after the Serving King with unshakable trust in Him from whom *all things* rise. It is they who will ride across the seas with Him time and time again, storm after storm. It is they who are HIs glory, simply because they have chosen to continue to chase after the Serving King even in the midst of the fiercest storm...

Day 111

TOLLGATE

"Great achievement is usually born of great sacrifice, and is never the result of selfishness." —Napoleon Hill

I appeal to you therefore, brothers, by the mercies of God, to present your bodies as a living sacrifice, holy and acceptable to God, which is your spiritual worship..
(Romans 12:1)

The early days of the quest after the Serving King are often filled with dreams of heaven, life in the hereafter, the joy of right relationship with God in this *present condition*. But sooner or later, the quest returns to the mundane, day-to-day affairs, the challenge of living a *holy and acceptable* life in the right now. And the right now can be exceptionally challenging for those hampered by this *present condition*.

So arrives the *tollgate* in the trek after the Serving King, the startling recognition that the journey can go no further in this *present condition*. The *tollgate* mandates *sacrifice*, a necessary payment for those inclined to continue the journey in the quest after the Serving King. And yes, the *sacrifice* is expensive, a comprehensive surrendering of the flesh to the purposes of the Serving King.

But the body, long used to its comprehensive rule over every dimension of life, resists the sacrifice necessary to continue the chase after the Serving King. It screams, wailing, kicking, and screaming as you drag it to the altar, surrendering it the reign of the King. The body, engulfed in the throes of resistance, wrongly assumes the King will reject so noisy and uncooperative a body. But the King, long accustomed to the wailing of flesh, embraces your sacrifice, pulls it to Himself, whispering a calming beckoning as the body convulses at the tollgate of final surrender.

His acceptance of such an unworthy body renders it holy, another useful tool in the quest after the Serving King. The body, once a worthy foe to the desires of the King, now responds to His wooing, His challenge to mount up, to embrace the quest yet ahead. The grandest of 'whisperers', He woos the body into the quest. The enemy, the flesh, is now an ally in the chase after the Serving King...

Day 112

THE SQUEEZE

"Conformity is the jailer of freedom and the enemy of growth."
—John F. Kennedy

Do not be conformed to this world, but be transformed by the renewal of your mind, that by testing you may discern what is the will of God, what is good and acceptable and perfect.
(Romans 12:2)

N o one escapes the *squeeze*, culture's constant and persistent pressure to conform, to walk in the patterns determined appropriate by the ruling party of the moment. And so the *squeeze* as each moment fills with expectations, conformity mandated, predictable schema sanctioned by those in power. And no greater power than the ability to determine the patterns of the mind, for as one thinks, so does one act.

So comes the challenge to recognize the *squeezed mind* shaped by years of *squeezing*, careful and persistent shaping by those granted access to the mind. And once *squeezed*, the mind is slow to reshape, not nearly as pliable as some would like to imagine. Nonetheless, the call of the Serving King is clear, the mind must be *re-squeezed*, shaped anew by *replacing* old ways of thinking, old ways of *'being and doing'*.

And you will be tempted to retain some of the old ways of thinking, seasoned ways of *'being and doing'*, often tested, long trusted, difficult to release. But the trek after the Serving King can never move toward what is *acceptable and perfect* while dragging along old ways of thinking, pragmatic as they may be in the old ways of *'being and doing'*.

Thus, the *will of God* can never be found in the old ways of thinking. Instead, a new mind must be created, piece by piece, each carefully placed by the illumination of the Holy Spirit as the Word of God becomes clearer and clearer. And with each new insight comes the need to remove the old. Resist the temptation to simply make room for the *new* in the midst of the old. This is a major overhaul, a complete redo and no better time to start than the present. Chase on toward the new mind…

Day 113

STUCK...

"Treat a man as he is and he will remain as he is. Treat a man as he can and should be and he will become as he can and should be." —Stephen R. Covey

For by the grace given to me I say to everyone among you not to think of himself more highly than he ought to think, but to think with sober judgment, each according to the measure of faith that God has assigned.
(Romans 12:3)

The trek after the Serving King inevitably reaches an impasse, acceptance of the status quo, contentment with this present condition. Cloaked in false humility, the quest for *good, acceptable, and perfect* comes to a halt, resting on the foundation of *grace*. The saint, *thinking more highly than he ought*, confuses *grace*, God's acceptance of *this present condition*, broken and corrupt as it is, with God's contentment with *this present condition*. So arrogance cripples the call to carry on toward *good, acceptable, and perfect*. The arrogance of false humility cripples the saint, rendering the quest finished, the *good, acceptable, and perfect* abandoned and sacrificed in the name of *humility*.

But *sober judgment*, the ability to *see* this present condition in the reflection of what *"...can and should be,"* refuses to surrender the quest for *good, acceptable, and perfect*; instead, beckoning the paused saint *stuck in this present condition* to carry on, to trek farther down the trail, closer to the *good, acceptable, and perfect*. *Sober judgment* allows no one to wallow in brokenness, content in God's acceptance of *this present condition*.

Grace never treats *"...a man as he is"* but rather embraces this present condition with hope for what *"...he can and should be."* So sober judgment inspires the saint to carry on down the trail, refusing to think more highly than he ought, determined to actualize the measure of faith God has provided to carry on deeper and deeper into the trek after the Serving King.

Sober judgment embraces the measure of faith necessary to rise up from this present condition. The journey is not over, nor this present condition a final resting place. Sober judgment allows no one to be stuck. Chase on. There is still much ground to cover in the chase yet ahead...

Day 114

WRONG TRAIL...

"Form follows function—that has been misunderstood. Form and function should be one, joined in a spiritual union." —Frank Lloyd Wright

For as in one body we have many members, and the members do not all have the same function, so we, though many, are one body in Christ, and individually members one of another.
(Romans 12:4-5)

The novice, unfamiliar with the unique *trail* of every journeyer chasing after the Serving King, often becomes disoriented, confused by the many crossing trails of those chasing after the Serving King. Some, too timid to simply stay close on the heels of the Serving King, often meander off the intended *trail*, distracted by *trails* more appealing. And so, the *right trail* of another trekker becomes the *wrong trail* for anyone distracted by the sight of other trekkers and trails.

Wrong trails, well-worn paths of *'being and doing'* intended for another, litter the landscape as trekkers of all kinds remain on the heels of the Serving King functioning in precisely the manner intended by the Serving King. The novice, thinking all trekkers intended for the same path, often meanders down the *wrong right trail*, content to follow the *right trail* of another, a *trail* more appealing but a *wrong trail* nonetheless.

But the *body of Christ* is massive, a comprehensive organism, composed of countless trekkers each with a unique *form and function,* each enabling the *body* to thrive as it carries out the mission of the Serving King across a broad spectrum of responsibilities. And so, the novice is often tempted to take on the *form* of another trekker, to function in the manner of another, distracted by *form and function* designed for the trek of another follower of the King.

Fortunately, the Serving King is faithful to those who have set out after Him, and He is reliable in reminding all who trek after Him of their intended *form and function.* But *form and function* can only be found *"...in a Spiritual union."* So every trekker must stay in tune with the whisperings of the Spirit. Only in the Spirit can *form and function* avoid the crowd on well-intentioned *wrong trails...*

Day 115

NOT TALENT...

"What you are is God's gift to you, what you become is your gift to God."
—Hans Urs von Balthasar

Having gifts that differ according to the grace given to us, let us use them:
if prophecy, in proportion to our faith...
(Romans 12:6)

E very trekker embarks on the trek after the Serving King with talents and abilities inherited at birth, now honed and refined, ready for deployment along the way. And these talents, long trusted and dependable, will beckon to remain in use, reliable resources for the journey yet ahead. But such is not the way of the Serving King. Talents will often be a nuisance, clamoring for use in the place of the *gift,* hindering rather than helping in the quest after the Serving King.

But *gifts,* better yet, *spiritual gifts,* are rarely connected to talents and are essential to thriving in the quest after the Serving King. *Gifts,* unlike talents, are only operational as the Spirit enables and empowers, thereby creating a terrifying and unceasing dependence upon the Spirit. Nor will *gifts* mandate usage; instead, they wait patiently for *"...let us use them"* to actualize under the guidance and direction of those receiving the *gift.* Thus, each *gift* waits patiently to be used *"...in proportion to our faith."*

Tragically, those who fail to actualize their *gift* rob the *body* of much-needed components, crippling every effort to *be and do* as the Serving King mandates. Thus, the *body,* intended and equipped to stride robustly along the trail of the Serving King, limps pitifully along as *gifts* lay dormant, unused, wasted potential. Even more tragic is the contagious nature of *unused gifts,* spreading like wildfire across the body, burdening those parts still functioning to the breaking point. And so, the body of Christ limps to its destination, dragging *latent gifts.* But today is a new day, and, perhaps, this is the day the *gifts* find the light of day. Let us use them *in proportion to our faith...*

Day 116

VARIETY...

"Variety may be the spice of life, but consistency pays the bills."
—Doug Cooper

...if service, in our serving; the one who teaches, in his teaching; the one who exhorts, in his exhortation; the one who contributes, in generosity; the one who leads, with zeal; the one who does acts of mercy, with cheerfulness.
(Romans 12:7-8)

Variety is, indeed, the spice of life, but make no mistake, "...consistency pays the bills." And the bills need to be paid. But consistency has an unintended consequence slowly creeping into the life of those persistent in their trek after the Serving King: complacency. Complacency robs the *gift* of its *zeal and* cheerfulness, rendering the *gift* just another act of stifling legalism. And the many, thinking obedience of primary importance, will continue in the trek turning the *gift* into drudgery, lifeless acts, void of the passion so critical to any act of obedience to the Serving King.

Once void of passion, the *gifts* given to another begin to appeal, wooing the passionless trekker toward alternative ways of *'being and doing'*, tasks assigned to others. But lusting for variety, the spice of life, many will leave behind the assigned *gift*, longing for the trail of another's quest.

Still, there is another way, the way of the Serving King, embracing the gift with *zeal*, reckless abandon, infusing old ways of *'being and doing'* with life-giving passion. This is no mere *feeling*; rather, it is the determination of a fully-engaged *will*. So comes the call to completely engage, to leave behind *variety* with its passion of the moment, fickle and fading.

The *gift*, only possible through the indwelling of the Spirit, comes with a *passion* on demand, rooted in the abiding Spirit. Herein lies Paul's command to engage with the *zeal* made possible through the Spirit's abiding presence. The *passion of variety* will come and go, but His passion is available to all chasing after the Serving King. Seize the *gift*, fully engage, and *pay the bills*. Consistency is the lifeblood of those following the King.

Day 117

THE LONELY RACE...

*"Do your work with your whole heart, and you will succeed –
there's so little competition." —Elbert Hubbard*

*Let love be genuine. Abhor what is evil; hold fast to what is good. Love one
another with brotherly affection. Outdo one another in showing honor.
(Romans 12:9-10)*

Few in the trek after the Serving King take seriously Paul's challenge to *compete*, literally, to *outdo one another* in the quest to mimic the *'being and doing'* of the Serving King. Instead, the many charge ahead, cloaking desires to *get ahead* in verbiage aligned with serving the King. And so, *success* is too often shrouded as *blessing, God's blessing,* showered on the faithful, those who have succeeded in *outdoing* other competitors in the field, fellow trekkers determined to *outdo one another in showing honor.* But rarely does the blessing of God manifest in the icons of the world.

This is a *competition* of a very special kind, a self-surrendering of the highest kind, stripping all competitors of all worldly motivation, rendering this *competition* a race to the bottom, not the top. Hence, competitors are rarely rewarded with trophies of the world, distractions of the worst kind, burdening all competitors with prizes hindering those pursuing the trail of the Serving King. Trophies from the King are rarely seen by those hot on the heels of success.

The grand prize, awarded to the persistent few, consumes the *heart,* the *whole heart,* capturing it, sealing it in a passion for the Serving King. Winners care not for the trophies of this world, prizes fraught with privileges of every kind; instead, the *heart of flesh* rises out of the *heart of stone* consumed with a burning passion for God and God's people. The *heart aflame* is the grand prize for those *outdoing one another.*

Sadly, even within the community of faith "...there's so little competition." You may soon discover there are few to race against, too few competitors to notice, a wide-open course for those willing to compete in *the lonely race.* Fear not, there is yet one competitor up ahead blazing the trail of the Serving King...

Day 118

ACHIEVEMENT, NOT ACTIVITY...

"Don't mistake activity with achievement." —John Wooden

Do not be slothful in zeal, be fervent in spirit, serve the Lord.
(Romans 12:11)

Staying *active* in the trek after the Serving King is never problematic; however, one ought never confuse *activity* with achievement or, more importantly, activity with *serving the Lord*. Enthusiasts have long valued activity as the 'cornerstone' of being religious. Unfortunately, being religious is never the goal in the chase after the Serving King. Nonetheless, the community of faith is often filled with zealots consumed with staying busy, running here and there, flittering from project to project. And given the call to care for the needy, zealots in the faith often become social workers of the grandest kind, feeding the poor, clothing the naked, visiting the sick, all noble tasks in and of themselves. But key to all activity is the call of God, the reassurance this activity is what God would have you do in this present moment.

Content to simply stay busy, the many often lose sight of the calling of God and lose their way in the busyness of social work. But, in the end, the question ought to be asked, "What did we actually accomplish with all of our busyness? Were those we clothed brought any closer to a saving relationship with the Serving King? Did those we feed sense the presence of God, know that we are His servants, feeding others only because the Serving King asked us to do so?" Or have we simply become social workers, serving the poor rather than the Serving King who sends us? Have the saints simply become kind and good people?

The reward of activity often steals the more important, achievement. The latter, achievement, accomplishes precisely what God desires to be done. It liberates from the endless call of activity always available to those looking to stay busy. Achievement acknowledges the reality of God who calls, "Be still and know that I am God" (Psalm 46:10). And yes, God often calls those who hear Him into activity. But never confuse mere activity with achievement as you chase on...

Day 119

TEST TUBE...

"Wise are they who have learned these truths: Trouble is temporary. Time is tonic. Tribulation is a test tube." —William Arthur Ward

Rejoice in hope, be patient in tribulation, be constant in prayer.
(Romans 12:12)

The trail of the Serving King traverses across terrains of all kinds. Early in the trek, the Serving King, conscious of your inabilities, your frailties, meanders through the soft paths of the meadows allowing you to adjust to the chase on the heals of the Serving King. But with each passing day comes strength, newly-discovered abilities, stamina for tougher terrain. So comes the days designed to try your mettle, to determine if you are indeed ready for the more ardent paths of the Serving King. The trails ahead are truly the 'test tube' of your transformation.

Be warned, earlier paths, flat and cozy, required little spiritual discipline to navigate. They are purposely gentle, non-challenging, requiring only a willingness to walk on. But the trails ahead are trails of a different kind. These trails cannot be navigated without the basics, the foundational tools for all who would follow the Serving King across the steep mountains yet ahead. Hope is the footstool for all who desire to remain on the heels of the Serving King. It is the fruit of seeing the many, just like you, who have gone on before you. They delight in your presence, calling you to join the quest, to keep moving forward, even as the trail steepens before you. Understand, these trails will require more than you have, abilities and stamina only available to those feasting at the table of the Serving King. And yes, you will fall on these trails, sometimes wounding yourself, sometimes painfully.

So comes the need for prayer, the unleashing of God's power into your daily walk. Prayer empowers you for the journey yet ahead. You are discovering ways of 'being and doing' once unthinkable, far beyond the natural abilities you have depended on for years. But, be of good cheer, you are learning to succeed, to chase on in the 'test tube'. Look what you are becoming as you chase on...

Day 120

UNDERSTANDING...

"There is no hospitality like understanding." —Vanna Bonta

Contribute to the needs of the saints and seek to show hospitality.
(Romans 12:13)

Novices in the trek after the Serving King are full of wants and desires rooted in the old ways of *'being and doing', and* many novices begin the trek in hopes of securing resources to meet those wants and desires. Soon they too will discover the King is in the business of meeting *needs* not mere wants and desires, and there is a world of difference between the two. But the novice, unable to see the difference, often languishes along the trail, wondering why the Serving King, or at least His minions, are not rising to meet the *want of the moment*. And every moment is filled with *wants*.

Nonetheless, sooner or later, other trekkers, kind souls, equally in the early stages of transformation, *confuse* the *needs of the* saints with the *wants of the* saints. Rarely are the two congruent, but in steps the kind soul to fill the *want of the moment*. But feeding *wants* does little to abate the hunger. *Wants* have a hearty appetite. Hence, the need to clearly understand the *need* of the moment.

Learning the difference between the two is time-consuming, requiring intimate knowledge of *the saint*, for no two saints are ever built the same, ever at the same stage of development in the quest after the Serving King. Such knowledge can only be acquired in the time-consuming labor of walking alongside rookie trekkers.

Thus, *hospitality* always begins with understanding each *saint*, a time-ladened endeavor requiring a willingness to journey alongside those the King brings into your path. You will be tempted to simply meet the *want*, to provide resources, and quickly exit. But Godly hospitality knows no such streamlined approach to hospitality. Those chasing after the Serving King soon discover, "There is no hospitality like understanding." Look deeper. There is yet much left to *understand...*

Day 121

BADLANDS...

"It is better to light a candle than curse the darkness."
—Eleanor Roosevelt

Bless those who persecute you; bless and do not curse them.
(Romans 12:14)

The journey after the Serving King inevitably leads into the *badlands*, places where neither the Serving King nor His followers are welcomed, and *persecution,* often serious and persistent, follows. Hence, learning to cope with persistent *persecution* becomes essential for those determined to remain faithful in sustaining His way of *'being and doing'*, even in the badlands.

You will be tempted as the *persecution* intensifies to blow out the *candle* and replace it with a more apt tool, or, as someone once suggested, "It is better to light a flame thrower than curse the darkness." But such is not the way of the Serving King. Burning the village of your enemies to the ground is simply not His preferred mode of operation. And so comes the challenge to embrace His way of *'being and doing'*, "Father, forgive them for they know not what they do" (Luke 23:34).

Blessing those who *persecute you* remains easy in the early days of the trek, close to home, miles from the bad*lands* of the enemy. But soon He will lead into the *badlands*, close proximity to those who *persecute*, those who most need the grace of the Serving King. And as the persecutors embark on their task, the temptation to abandon the *blessing* mandated by the Serving King will intensify with each passing moment in the badlands. The candle will flicker in the prevailing darkness. Curses will climb up the throat, clamoring to escape into the fresh air, begging to come to your aid. But curses have no place in the trek after the Serving King.

There is radiating in you a power far greater than curses. It is the power of *blessing* unleashed through the Spirit of Him who works in the heart and mind of all persons. *Blessing* unleashes the power of God to accomplish what only the King can do in the *badlands*.

Day 122

EMPATHY...

*"Empathy begins with understanding life from another person's perspective.
Nobody has an objective experience of reality. It's all through our own
individual prisms." —Sterling K. Brown*

*Rejoice with those who rejoice, weep with those who weep.
(Romans 12:15)*

B lessing one's enemy is one thing, rejoicing with them quite another, but as
you have come to expect, His way of *'being and doing'* ushers in an entirely
new way of your 'being and doing'. And never more so than the ability to have
authentic empathy for others in your life, both friend and foe. Empathy toward
enemies is one of the final fruits in the trek after the Serving King, available only
to those who courageously stay on the trek as the Serving King elevates into the
highest regions.

Breaking free from your 'individual prism' is a difficult task. Few truly succeed, hence, so little authentic empathy in the world. Still, the Serving King, via
incarnation, truly models what it means to step into another individual's 'prism',
to genuinely understand the struggles of what it means to be human. But having
done so, He truly comprehends what it means to be one of us, to battle the
raging infection with which we all must contend.

So comes the challenge to understand the perspective of another, even your
enemy. But understanding is never enough; rather, it simply opens the door, creating the possibility of genuinely rejoicing with those who rejoice and weeping
with those who weep. And it is this authentic comprehension allowing enemies
to truly communicate, creating pathways for meaningful peace.

Those who genuinely laugh together, weep together, rarely find cause for
war. Instead, pathways of understanding create lasting peace as friend and foe
alike find trinkets of commonality, uniting even the most divergent of peoples.
But genuine understanding requires time and lots of it. Slow down long enough
to hear the 'prism' of those who oppose you, even those who war against you.
And you will know you have heard enough when laughter fills the air and tears
flow down your cheeks. Until then, talk on as you chase after the Serving King...

Day 123

NON-THINKING...

*"How is it they live in such harmony the billions of stars—when most men can
barely go a minute without declaring war in their minds
about someone they know." —Thomas Aquinas*

*Live in harmony with one another. Do not be haughty,
but associate with the lowly. Never be wise in your own sight.
(Romans 12:16)*

T he stars, at least as far as we know, have a huge advantage over those chasing
after the Serving King; they do not *think*, and so the secret to living in harmony. Stars spend no time considering which one burns the brightest, which one
is the largest, or even the oldest. They simply burn day after day illuminating
the darkness in every direction, never concerned with the proficiency of the star
next door. There is much to be learned from stars...

Unfortunately, humanity's greatest gift, the ability to think, is also its greatest
liability, stealing harmony from even the ranks of those chasing after the Serving
King. *Thinking* enables the creation of standards, measuring rods, tools of distinction assigning value to this or that person or thing. And once *valued*, the war to
be and acquire the valuable is relentless, a constant pursuit of more value. And
only in Him can enough *value* be found.

But *thinking* is a two-way street, equally proficient at destroying even the
most creative measuring rods. *Thinking* is capable of removing the temptation to
be wise in your own sight. *Thinking* liberates us to *burn brightly for the Serving
King* in places never before considered, to *associate with the lowly*. Thinking
unlocks doors to adventures in new and exciting places.

Still, in the end, *thinking* is only a tool, a means to an end, driven by the
self-determining *will*. And therein lies the battle, the challenge to *never be
haughty*, to unleash His way of *'being and doing'* into the deepest fathoms of
self. Only the redeemed self can challenge the mind to *think* in the ways of the
Serving King. This is not a time for *non-thinking* but, rather, *thinking* illuminated
by the Bright Morning Star as you chase on...

Day 124

IT'S ON YOU…

"Pray like it all depends on God, but work like it all depends on you."
—Dave Ramsey

Repay no one evil for evil, but give thought to do what is honorable in the sight of all. If possible, so far as it depends on you, live peaceably with all.
(Romans 12:17-18)

Peace thrives in solitude, no competing voices for how this or that ought to be done. Instead, just one voice, a single decision-maker, a solitary soul dictating the course ahead. But the Serving King has little patience for the life of solitude, insisting instead on life in community, the messiness of others. And life with others would be easy enough, if others would simply play nice, behave as you expect them to. But, alas, communal life is rarely neat and clean. To the contrary, communal life is more times than not messy and uncomfortable. Wounds are a simple reality for those living with messy others. Oh, the temptation to cut and run, to avoid the trauma and drama of living with others.

Unintentional wounds are the by-product of rubbing shoulders with others. As the saying goes, "Life happens." Forgiveness of 'shoulder rubbing' is child's play compared to dealing with 'evil', intentional malice toward others. Evil unleashed within community creates a knee-jerk reaction in many people, if not most. Evil evokes evil, creating an endless cycle of retribution, each new act generating rage in the victim soon to be the aggressor. So comes the challenge to break the cycle, to step into His ways of 'being and doing', to repay evil in ways yet unknown and untried.

It is the 'give thought' which creates the hesitation, the pause, prior to any counteract. 'Give thought' requires patience, careful reflection, interaction with the Serving King, the only opinion that really matters. Only He knows the path to 'honorable', that which God would have you to do in the face of evil. To 'give thought' is to pause and ask the question, "Father, what would be the honorable thing to do in light of this evil?" Only when He has spoken, dare you respond to the evil amongst the people of God. Chase on carefully…

Day 125

NEVER...

"Vengeance, retaliation, retribution, revenge are deceitful brothers; vile, beguiling demons promising justifiable compensation to a pained soul for his losses. Yet in truth they craftily fester away all else of worth remaining."
—Richelle E. Goodrich

Beloved, never avenge yourselves, but leave it to the wrath of God, for it is written, "Vengeance is Mine, I will repay, says the Lord."
(Romans 12:19)

Never is a big word, comprehensive, consuming every excuse it encounters. *Never* has no patience for excuses, even those most justified, most relevant, most reasonable in a world void of justice. *Never* is permanent, a static condition, mandating obedience by all those chasing deepest into the quest after the Serving King. *Never* refuses to sleep, always persistent on its watch...

But the trek after the Serving King is a pragmatic quest liberated from legalism; instead, it's enhanced by a stream of invitations enabling all who embrace them to reach the steepest parts of the trail. *His never* comes in the form of an invitation to *His beloved*, those whom He cares for most. *His never* beckons His followers to embrace yet again His way of *'being and doing'*. *His never* is reserved for those whose love compels them to levels of obedience only imagined by *the many*.

And yes, *His vengeance*, as you might have guessed, looks nothing like the vengeance of this world. *His vengeance* hangs on the cross of the Serving King, bloodied and crushed, exacting *His vengeance* as redemption sweeps the land, even upon those who crushed Him, "...Father forgive them for they know not what they do" (Luke 23:34). And those most faithful in embracing the trek of the Serving King will also know the vengeance of the Father, a cross of their very own, a redemptive moment sweeping the landscape, likewise crushing those courageous enough to embrace the *never* of the Serving King.

The *cross* is the vengeance of the Lord, His way of *'being and doing'* in a world void of His ways. Only in the cross do the *beguiling demons* suffer ultimate defeat, destruction at the foot of the cross. And those who miss the *never* will soon discover how "... they craftily fester away all else worth remaining." Chase on...

Day 126

THE HEAP...

*"Fertilizer does no good in a heap, but a little spread around
works miracles all over." —Richard Brinsley Sheridan*

*To the contrary, "if your enemy is hungry, feed him; if he is thirsty, give him
something to drink; for by so doing you will heap burning coals on his head."
(Romans 12:20)*

N ever avenging oneself seems reasonable, enough, a manageable standard for those chasing on the heels of the Serving King. But remaining on His heels becomes increasingly difficult with each new unveiling of His way of *'being and doing'*, and none more demanding than the call to *"feed him...give him something to drink."* The *him* is the most dangerous of all persons, one's enemy. Nonetheless, caring for your enemy is the final grade, the steepest climb, the finish line, for those intent on chasing with Him till the end, the very end, where nothing is left to surrender.

So the *vengeance of God* takes on new meaning in a life committed to mimicking His way of *'being and doing'*. Gone are the world's weapons of vengeance, swords and guns, violence and destruction. In their place, the *burning coals* of God's vengeance, food and drink to those in need, kindness undeserved, unmerited by any standard but God's. Only God would dare to proclaim *heaping burning coals on his head (the enemy)* in the unleashing of kindness and *grace.*

And so the challenge to God's people to create and sustain the *heap,* a massive unleashing of the vengeance of God, *food and drink* in abundance, unmerited compassion and concern for those inflicting pain and chaos toward the people of God. Few join Him in creating the *heap, unleashing divine vengeance* in a world of violence, a culture unaccustomed to *grace.* Few will bring their *food and drink* to the enemies of the land.

Tragically, the *heap* rarely forms; instead, it remains illusive and invisible as the *Church* resists the *vengeance of God,* the *burning coals* of the King. With Peter, swords (words) fly, bloodletting continues, the pleas of the Serving King ignored, "Put your sword back into its place. For all who take the sword will perish by the sword" (Matthew 26:52). Chase on...

Day 127

THE ENEMY'S ACHILLES' HEEL...

"You've injured me, Farshooter, most deadly of the gods; And I'd punish you,
if I had the power." —Homer (The Iliad)

Do not be overcome by evil, but overcome evil with good.
(Romans 12:21)

E vil has an *Achilles' heel* rarely shot by modern *Farshooters,* too schooled in the ways of the world to embrace His ways of *'being and doing'.* The enemy's *Achilles' heel* has long been visible by those chasing after the Serving King. But evil entrenches its way of *'being and doing'* into the fabric of the culture, a persistent thread woven into the unconscious collective mind, preventing a serious attempt to attack the enemy's Achilles' heel with the *good.*

Scripture warns of evil's lavish attempt to *"...bruise His heel"* (Genesis 3:14), violence of the worst kind, only to discover the Serving King has no *Achilles' heel,* even in a feigned moment of defeat. But *evil* knows no such luxury. Instead, *evil* writhes in the presence of *good,* His way of *'being and doing',* precision arrows from the quill of those chasing closest to the Serving King. Fortunately for *evil,* too few chasing after Him ever discover a new way of *'being and doing',* resorting over and over again to old and tired patterns of retribution, attempts to war against *evil* with tools *evil* knows all too well.

Tragically, like old briar rabbit, those chasing after the Serving King resort to *throwing evil into the briar patch* only to discover *evil* thrives in the thicket of thorns, blossoms in the ways of the world, retribution merely feeding the beast. The *good,* the only weapon *evil truly* fears, too often remains dormant, tucked away for enemies less serious than *evil.*

So comes the challenge to abandon the weapons of the world, to engage the *good,* His way of *'being and doing',* capable of defeating *evil* once and for all. All other weapons will fall short. Only the *good* can overcome *evil.* Whom amongst us will fight the evil giant armed only with the stone of goodness? Chase on into the fight ahead...

Day 128

THE AUTHORITY OF INTIMACY...

"To punish me for my contempt for authority,
fate made me an authority myself." —Albert Einstein

Let every person be subject to the governing authorities. For there is no
authority except from God, and those that exist have been instituted by God.
(Romans 13:1)

There is no greater threat to *institutional authority*, be it governments or written code, than *intimacy* with the Serving King, *life in the Spirit*. And not just any kind of *intimacy*, rather, the *intimacy of hearing*, knowing the voice of the Serving King; more than that, understanding His directions for life and praxis. Such intimacy knows no authority other than the voice of the Serving King. His beckoning sets the direction and purpose for every dimension of life. He is a God of the micros, the tiniest details of everyday life. His voice is *the authority of intimacy...*

The many, void of such *intimacy*, are left to *governing authorities*, aides to the deaf, those incapable of hearing the voice of the King. Theirs is a world of rules and regulations written by others for the deaf, stifling legalism, doldrums of the worst kind. Such authority governs the deaf attempting to create safe and secure environments for all who hear not the *intimate* voice of the Serving King. And so, Einstein's inglorious dilemma. Filled with contempt for those *authorities for the deaf,* he found himself under the authority of one, a lone rebel, isolated from the voice of the Serving King, lacking the *intimacy* that guides.

Nonetheless, there is another way to journey, sheltered in the *intimacy of the Serving King*. But beware of this *intimacy* with the Serving King. Such *intimacy* is costly and often lonely. He rarely, if ever, speaks intimately to the throngs; instead, He whispers in the ear of His beloved. And only those who *hear* His whispers dare wander off the trail of the many, the path of the governed, the worn-out trail.

But rest assured, there is no loneliness for those who wander off the worn-out trail of the governed while chasing on the heels of the Serving King. No better companionship can be found as you chase on...

Day 129

DO GOOD...

"We have not to crown the exceptional man who knows he can rule; rather we must crown the much more exceptional man who knows he can't."
—G.K. Chesterton

Therefore whoever resists the authorities resists what God has appointed, and those who resist will incur judgment. For rulers are not a terror to good conduct, but to bad. Would you have no fear of the one who is in authority? Then do what is good, and you will receive His approval...
(Romans 13:2-3)

The call to *do the good* ought never be confused with a blanket approval of the whims of those in authority. To the contrary, Paul clearly provides the measuring rod for determining whether an authority is of God or simply installed by the whims of humanity: "...do what is good, and you will receive His approval." So the lightening rod for those in authority. Do they approve of the 'good', God's will, being done by those chasing after the Serving King?

But good is elusive, difficult to identify at times, too often linked to the approval of the majority, those in power. Good ought to be linked to the *'will of God'*, the undeniable assurance that God has called you to act in a specific way, His way of 'being and doing'. Good is simply doing what God has called you to do. Peter and John faced the difficult challenge of remaining faithful to the calling of God when reproached by those in authority.

John, like Peter, was told by the Sanhedrin not to preach in the name of Jesus, and he replied, *"Judge for yourselves whether it is right in God's sight to obey you rather than God"* (Acts 4:19). Upon being released, they resumed their work and, consequently, were taken into custody. To the charge of the Sanhedrin that they had filled Jerusalem with their teaching, they replied, *"We must obey God rather than man!"* (Acts 5:29). So comes the opportunity to determine if the authority is of God. Will the Sanhedrin affirm their actions to scold them yet again?

Resisting authorities, civil disobedience, is a difficult path to walk. But, rest assured, if you do what is right, the authorities above you will be held accountable for their evaluation. Will they give you approval or surrender God's appointment? Either way, chase on...

Day 130

DO WRONG...

"There are only two forces in the world, the sword and the spirit. In the long run the sword will always be conquered by the spirit."
—Napoleon Bonaparte

...for he is God's servant for your good. But if you do wrong, be afraid,
for he does not bear the sword in vain. For he is the servant of God,
an avenger who carries out God's wrath on the wrongdoer.
(Romans 13:4)

Like the good, the wrong, correlates not to written legal but, rather, the much more demanding whispers of the Spirit etched in the heart and mind of those chasing after the Serving King. Nor can obedience of the heart, the appropriate response to the whispering Spirit, be mandated by swords. Swords are the realm of civil obedience, the mundane of life, the trivialization of obedience, speed limits, lawsuits, and other matters of communal life easily regulated by the threat of violence. The sword can indeed bring its power to bear on such externals of mundane living, but its power has no relevance for the heart. Only the Spirit of the Serving King can conquer the unruly heart destined to do wrong.

The sword, impotent in matters of the heart, can do nothing to conquer the raging heart, the rebellious spirit. Such is the domain of the Spirit, the power of God made manifest in the conquered heart. But the sword can manipulate external obedience, a tragic trivializing of the wooing of the Spirit. Such obedience moves only in the shallows of reality, hiding the raging heart, the rebellious spirit lurking in the heart. So the rebellious spirit conquers the sword reigning in the heart, ignoring all threats from the sword. Just as Bonaparte suggested long ago, "...in the long run the sword will always be conquered by the Spirit."

But the Spirit, long accustomed to reigning in the heart, has met its match as the Spirit of God declares war, a battle for control deep in the heart, the ultimate reality. Here, there is no trivial obedience. Here, there are no swords to inflict wrath. Here, is the ultimate contest, the battle for supremacy, control of the heart. In the end, there are indeed only two forces in the world, the spirit and His Spirit. He will not slay your spirit. Only surrender can bring this battle to a close as you chase on...

Day 131

THERE COMES A TIME...

"There comes a time when one must take a position that is neither safe, nor politic, nor popular, but he must take it because conscience tells him it is right."
—Martin Luther King Jr.

Therefore one must be in subjection, not only to avoid God's wrath but also for the sake of conscience.
(Romans 13:5)

You will be tempted to think, *"There comes a time..."* is an everyday occurrence, a divine-initiated right, a trump card available for play whenever needed, but it is not. Instead, *"There comes a time..."* is a rarity in life reserved for those moments when the trek after the Serving King takes a path that is *neither safe, nor politic, nor popular*. But *"There comes a time..."* is not a *do as you please card* deployed when convenient in the throes of communal living. Instead, it is the domain of *Spirit-initiated* civil disobedience, an atypical moment in the quest after the Serving King. And it is always neither safe nor politic.

Hence, the challenge of communal living can be exhausting at times. Many are tempted to enjoy the *benefits* of civil community while ignoring the inconvenience of compliance for the sake of others. But communal living always mandates *authorities,* those positioned to ensure *fairness* for all those present within the community. Thus, communal living often requires the surrendering of personal privilege for the sake of the community, and so life in the Spirit typically syncs with communal authorities, those in place to oversee communal life, communal synchronization, peace for a broad range of interconnected persons.

Therefore, life in community requires a willingness to *be in subjection,* sometimes at the most inopportune times. And *subjection* to others at inopportune times rarely comes easily; instead, more times than not, *subjection* is a fruit of the Spirit, an empowering to surrender personal wants and privileges for the sake of others. *Subjection* is the foundation of all communal living, from governments to homeowners associations. But it is always messy, inconsistent, costly, and unpredictable for even seasoned saints in the trek. Conscience rarely leads toward civil disobedience, rather, more often taking the steepest trail on the chase after the Serving King...

Day 132

MERE TAXES...

"I like to pay taxes. With them, I buy civilization"
—Oliver Wendell Holmes Jr.

For because of this you also pay taxes,
for the authorities are ministers of God, attending to this very thing.
(Romans 13:6)

Taxes, in all shapes and sizes, are mere inconveniences, trivial in comparison to the cost of chasing after the Serving King. The early stages, the steps of beginners, stay clear of *offering plates* of all kinds, thinking the journey after the Serving King to be free of taxes, a toll-free road. And, indeed, it can be for the novice.

But the journey rarely remains costless for those determined to pay any price to remain close on the heels of the Serving King. Sooner rather than later, costs begin to appear, mere nuisances at first, small *pocket change*, hardly noticeable in the coffers of the King. Little attention is given to the distribution of mere *pocket change* as the Serving King offers His resources to those undeserving, and, yes, any recipient is undeserving. But the Serving King is never content with mere *pocket change*, trivial *taxes* to those with abundance, more than is needed to implement His way of *'being and doing'*.

And so, the discovery of just how little is needed to implement His way of *'being and doing'* as one migrates farther and farther down the trail of the Serving King. Gone is the lust for more of *this and that*. In its place, contentment with the leftovers, resources unused by the King.

But for those deepest in the quest after the Serving King, a new way of *'being and doing'* radically transforms every attitude toward giving for the sake of the Kingdom of God. Gone is the mundane concept of *buying civilization* and, in its place, the privilege of *buying salvation* for those most in need. And this is no mere *tax*, a pittance of available resources; rather, it is the glory of *stewardship*, micromanager of the King's resources in your hands. And so, you have become *ministers of God* as you chase on...

Day 133

OWED...

"I decided to devote my life to telling the story because I felt that having survived I owe something to the dead. and anyone who does not remember betrays them again." —Elie Wiesel

Pay to all what is owed to them: taxes to whom taxes are owed, revenue to whom revenue is owed, respect to whom respect is owed, honor to whom honor is owed.
(Romans 13:7)

Survivors, those who have discovered the lifeline of the King, initially sense a debt to the *still dead*, those lingering in the old ways of *'being and doing'*. And the debt owed them comes from the lips of the Serving King, "Go therefore and make disciples of all nations, baptizing them in the name of the Father and of the Son and of the Holy Spirit" (Matthew 28:19). It is the very purpose for His coming and His invitation to follow, to trek after Him as He remembers the *still dead*.

But remembering the debt never comes easy for the living, liberated from the land of the *walking dead,* freed from the old ways of *'being and doing'*. Once liberated, the living delight in life anew, changes so profound and meaningful. The *still dead* often have no interest in the *living* and their new ways of *'being and doing'*. And so, the living often lose interest in returning to the lands of the *still dead*. Spurned and rejected too often for comfort, those lands and its inhabitants no longer appeal to the *living*. Great is the temptation to remain in the company of the now *living*.

But the Serving King never loses sight of those *still dead*, still lost in the ways of the world. They are *beloved* as well, like all of His children, driving the Serving King to return to their lands over and over again via the hands and feet of those chasing closest to Him. His passion for them becomes the *debt of His followers* as they embrace His passions and His concerns.

So comes the determination to *pay to all what is owed them*. It is the challenge of the Serving King to all who would trek after Him. And as Ellie Wiesel understood so well, "...anyone who does not remember them betrays them again." Chase on...

Day 134

LAW FULFILLED...

*"Being deeply loved by someone gives you strength, while loving someone
deeply gives you courage." —Lao Tzu*

*Owe no one anything, except to love each other,
for the one who loves another has fulfilled the law.
(Romans 13:8)*

C.S. Lewis wrote, "To love at all is to be vulnerable. Love anything and your heart will be wrung and possibly broken. If you want to make sure of keeping it intact you must give it to no one, not even an animal. Wrap it carefully round with hobbies and little luxuries; avoid all entanglements." Sadly, most of us learn this lesson far too soon, crippling our ability to love, even when chasing after the Serving King. The antidote, found only in the indwelling presence of the Holy Spirit, empowers the wounded to love, to accept the risk of another broken heart, to embrace the challenge to fulfill the law simply by loving another. It is His way of 'being and doing'.

The highest portions of the trail mandate a profound sense of love. You simply will not have the courage to carry on unless empowered by a love of God and neighbor. But this love is not generated by those chasing after the Serving King. To the contrary, this love, His love, simply arrives as the Spirit takes up residence in every believer. Love like this is the fruit of His presence, the unexpected reward of reaching the higher plateaus in this quest after the Serving King.

Likewise, the courage to execute, to carry out His outlandish love, is the by-product of the Spirit as well. Radical self-sacrifice no longer terrifies the lover; rather, now fully in love, the lover embraces every challenge of self-sacrifice, gladly surrendering all needs for the sake of the beloved. This love knows no bounds, fears no sacrifice. It is the abiding gift of the Holy Spirit. Others, not understanding your relentless courage, will shake their heads in wonder, marveling at the foolishness of your love for another. But you are only doing what love mandates must be done. You are fulfilling the law as you chase on...

Day 135

SUMS IT UP...

"Life it is not just a series of calculations and a sum total of statistics, it's about experience, it's about participation, it is something more complex and more interesting than what is obvious." —Daniel Libeskind

For the commandments, "You shall not commit adultery, You shall not murder, You shall not steal, You shall not covet," and any other commandment, are summed up in this word: "You shall love your neighbor as yourself." (Romans 13:9)

Unfortunately, hearing the particulars, the specific details needed to move forward on the trail of the Serving King, often remain unheard in the blazing speed of the modern quest. Life is simply too hectic at times to pause for directions, and so a course of action is unclear in the immediacy of the moment, filled as it is with options of every kind. But sometimes decisions need to be made in this very moment, ignorant or not of the needed details for the wisest course to follow. In the rushed moments of life, a philosophy of life is required to guide in the moment, a philosophy that *sums it up.* Fortunately, the Serving King provides just such a philosophy to guide and direct in those moments of uncertainty.

The particulars all depend on the *sums it up,* the foundation upon which all particulars, the *shall* and the *shall nots* stand. And so arrives the principle of *love your neighbor as yourself.* But loving your neighbor as yourself can be tricksy for those poorly suited for loving self. As Libeskind suggests, *"...it is something more complex and more interesting than what is obvious."*

This is no mere hedonism, a free-for-all of self-fulfillment, driven by the old ways of *'being and doing',* the slavery of the flesh, appetites ignorant of what is authentically good and helpful. No, this is a love likened to the ways of the Serving King, a self-sacrificial love consumed with what is best for the *other.* It is the way of the cross, His way, the Via Dolorosa, the way of suffering, for the sake of another. It is indeed *more interesting than what is obvious.* Love *sums it up.* It is the foundation upon which all particulars must stand as you chase on...

Day 136

PICK AND CHOOSE...

"The Bible tells us to love our neighbors, and also to love our enemies; probably because generally they are the same people." —G.K. Chesterton

Love does no wrong to a neighbor; therefore love is the fulfilling of the law..
(Romans 13:10)

The trek after the Serving King would be so much easier if we could choose those who journey with us, and moderns, mobile and free, are constantly tempted to do that very thing, pick and choose. The choosing, quiet and discreet, allows moderns to inconspicuously slip away into the night, freed from all responsibility of fulfilling the law of love toward less than ideal neighbors.

But the Body of Christ offers no such effortless mobility, the freedom to carefully pick and choose neighbors easily loved; instead, the Body of Christ makes enemies neighbors, inviting the rejected and abused to come and dine at the table of the Serving King. Only at the table of the Serving King are all welcome, even the dreaded enemy. The Body of Christ makes no distinctions between Jew and Gentile, master and slave, enemy and friend. To the contrary, all are welcome, all provided opportunity to be loved and cared for by those chasing deepest along the trail of the Serving King.

Nonetheless, you will be tempted to quietly slip away into the night, freed from the annoying neighbor, the gathering of the unpleasant, the throng of the difficult ones. It is the ever-present temptation to find new neighbors, lovable and pleasant, easy to love. But, such is not the way of the Serving King. His is the way of loving every neighbor, even the least of these, the most annoying of these.

So those in the community of the Serving King soon discover, "...they are the same people." And His way of 'being and doing' mandates love of neighbor, any neighbor, even your neighbor. And yes, moving would do no good. There, too, will be new neighbors just like the old neighbors, people needing the love and care found only in the community of those chasing after the Serving King...

Day 137

WAKE-UP...

"All dream, but not equally. Some dream by night in the dusty recesses of their minds, wake in the day to find that it was vanity: but the dreamers of the day are dangerous men, for they may act on their dreams with open eyes, making them possible." —T.E. Lawrence

Besides this you know the time, that the hour has come for you to wake from sleep. For salvation is nearer to us now than when we first believed. The night is far gone; the day is at hand. So then let us cast off the works of darkness and put on the armor of light.
(Romans 13:11-12)

Everyone sleeps, a much-needed cessation, ushering in healing to both mind and body. Those chasing deepest into the quest after the Serving King often require periods of respite, a reprieve from the intensity of the quest after the Serving King. This quest requires much sleep. But sleep creates its own world, a place of safety liberated from the harshness of reality, a world where even nightmares slip harmlessly away into the recesses of forgotten yesterdays. Such is the joy of sleep. And great is the temptation to simply sleep life away, hidden from the call to *be and do* in the ways of the Serving King.

But sleep is never meant to be a way of life, a numbed wandering through life, a shell-shocked stumbling through the difficult days of reality. To the contrary, sleep prepares and equips for life, even a difficult life, even a life devoted to chasing after the Serving King. So comes the challenge to *wake from sleep* as salvation draws near.

There is much yet to do as the return of the King is close. The residue of the old ways of *'being and doing'* still lingers, manifesting in the dreams of the sleeper, reminding the sleeper of days gone by, familiar ways of *thinking, 'being and doing'*. But now is the time to *cast off the works of darkness and put on the armor of light*.

Sleepers need no armor tucked safe and sound in the world of make-believe, nestled away from the trauma awaiting those daring to join the ranks of the day-dreamers, those who "*...act on their dreams with open eyes, making them possible.*" It is those fully awake, dressed in the *armor of light*, who dare to change their world, to usher in the Kingdom of the Serving King. Wake up sleeper and change the world as you chase on...

Day 138

WISHFUL THINKING…

"The best training program in the world is absolutely worthless without the will to execute it properly, consistently, and with intensity."
—John Romaniello

Let us walk properly as in the daytime, not in orgies and drunkenness, not in sexual immorality and sensuality, not in quarreling and jealousy.
(Romans 13:13)

Anyone can go for a *stroll* with the Serving King, peaceful meandering in the cool of the evening, pleasant conversations exploring the possibilities of what lies ahead for the brave of heart, the courageous, the conversational day-dreamers. Such are the early stages of *grace.* And great will be the temptation to remain on the occasional *stroll* with Serving King, daydreaming about what could be, if and when a decision were made to *walk properly*, to abandon the old ways of *'being and doing'.* But the old ways are deeply engrained, much deeper than we have imagined, habits clinging tightly to any and every tidbit of the old you. New *being* rarely easily translates into new *doing.*

But the Serving King has already equipped you for a new way of *'being and doing'*, a state-of-the-art *being* now installed, ready to implement an unfamiliar way of *doing,* His way. Now is the time to unleash His way of *'being and doing'*, to make real the wishful conversations of earlier strolls, to demand the *flesh* conform to the *being* the King has installed deep within you.

Still, new *being* must be actualized, unleashed to *be and do* in the ways of the King. And all *"…the best training program in the world is absolutely worthless without the will to execute."* Without the *will, new being* remains entrapped in *wishful thinking* as the old ways of doing rage on, refusing to surrender to mere *wishing thinking.* And so, the *new being* remains entrapped, polluted by old ways, *"…sexual immorality and sensuality, quarreling, and jealousy." Wishful thinking* remains, but the *will to execute* too often remains dormant, just below the sur-face of actuality. Thus, *wishful thinkers* continue to *stroll* with the Serving King. Perhaps, today is the day to finally *walk properly* as you chase on…

Day 139

PROVISIONS...

*"Human brutes, like other beasts, find snares and poison in the provision of life,
and are allured by their appetites to their destruction."*
—Jonathan Swift

*But put on the Lord Jesus Christ,
and make no provision for the flesh, to gratify its desires.*
(Romans 13:14)

The early stages of the trek after the Serving King has minimal requirements, mandating few lifestyle adjustments as one strolls through the *come as you are* stages of grace. But for those who trek deeper into the quest, much deeper than the novice even considers, lifestyle adjustments are required, necessary for those wanting to trek closest to the King. The trail ahead leaves no room for peripherals, unessential ways of *'being and doing'*, old core values no longer relevant or helpful for the course just ahead on the heels of the Serving King.

But the *flesh*, the old king, has an immense appetite and is accustomed to eating at will, a glutton whose appetite never abates. The old trails offered multiple meals along the way, feasts of every kind, an endless array of refreshments. And so, the *flesh* ruled the day, rendering you ill-equipped for bold adventures into the way of holiness, His way of *'being and doing'*. The *flesh* eats to its own destruction, a reckless suicide mission, a path of ruin for all who tread down its steep decay.

Fortunately, He comes to rescue, to redeem those far into the process of decay. He offers a way out, another way to *be and do*, even for those most lethargic, the most corroded by the decay of the *flesh*. He offers a way home, a way back to the days of youth, the way of redemption and healing for those tired of decay and ruin.

But the trail ahead knows no such snacks, no occasional visits to the old ways of *'being and doing'*, no sneaking just a taste of this or that. The trail ahead makes *no provision for the flesh,* none, not even an occasional tidbit. Still, the appetite of the *flesh* rages on, demanding you abandon the quest after the Serving King. Ignore the *flesh*. Let it die. Put on the *Lord Jesus Christ* and chase on...

145

Day 140

PESKY OPINIONS...

"The greatest deception men suffer is from their own opinions."
—Leonardo DaVinci

As for the one who is weak in faith, welcome him,
but not to quarrel over opinions.
(Romans 14:1)

Opinions litter the landscape surrounding the trail of the Serving King, unavoidable consequences of thinking out loud, polluting the trail with hard-earned sentiments left behind, markers for the *weak in faith*. *Opinions* are unintended consequences of conversations with the Serving King, moments of revelation, insight into His ways of *'being and doing'* designed uniquely for you. But novices, even extremely experienced novices, feel the urge to share newly-acquired insights, confident all other trekkers would benefit from their glorious insights from the Serving King.

So revelation, powerful and energizing, difficult to contain, bursts forth from the brain, pushing its way down the throat, gaining momentum, kicking the tongue into motion, anxious to catapult itself into the open air, accessible to ears of every kind. And the novice, misunderstanding the role of revelation, unique and personal, guidelines on *'being and doing'* intended for one, allows freshly-minted revelation to fly into the open air, polluting the trail for those who will follow. Tragically, revelation for one soon becomes little more than *opinion,* custom *'being and doing'* unleashed in the public square.

Quarrels are rarely far behind on a trail littered with *opinions*. They, too, are the unintended consequences of authentic encounters with the Serving King. Novices, unawares of the personal nature of all revelation, simply cannot resist the temptation to set free revelation from encounters with the Serving King. And so appears the final unintended consequence, collateral damage never envisioned by those determined to quarrel, to make known personal revelation, custom convictions from the Serving King: *the weak in faith* lose the trail of the Serving King. Distracted by quarrels of every kind, the *weak in faith* stumble on His trail as the Serving King moves on. It's not too late. Kick away the litter. The trail is still before you as you chase on...

Day 141

TABLE GUESTS...

*"I don't want any vegetables, thank you. I paid for the cow
to eat them for me." —Douglas Coupland*

*One person believes he may eat anything, while the weak person eats only
vegetables. Let not the one who eats despise the one who abstains,
and let not the one who abstains pass judgment on the one who eats,
for God has welcomed him.*
(Romans 14:2-3)

Novices are often, perhaps always, shocked by those welcomed by the King to His table. Even seasoned trekkers raise an eyebrow on occasion, surprised by the latest arrivals, ragged and brazen, worn out from life, hardly cleaned up enough to sit at the table of the King. But there they are, hobnobbing with the King, "...*for God has welcomed him.*"

The confusion is easy to understand. While the King welcomes all who would come to His Table, He rarely leaves anyone at the table in the same condition in which they arrived. It simply is not His way. It is not the way of *grace.* Thus, the well-groomed, regenerated, and redeemed soon wake up in the illusion of *always having been this way.* But nothing could be farther from the truth. All newcomers to the table of the King arrive in the same condition, filthy and unworthy, uncouth and ill-mannered. But, oh, how quickly *grace* erases the memory of days gone by. Forgetfulness is also a fruit of *grace.*

It is easy to forget the "...*the cow ate them for me.*" No one comes to the table of the King on their own merit. To the contrary, only by the *grace of the Serving King* does anyone gain access to the table of the King. He has eaten the vegetables for all who would dream to eat at the table of the King.

It is one of the great mysteries of the Kingdom of God, the privilege of feasting as you like and passing on those items too distasteful for consumption. Such is the nature of *grace,* for the Serving King has eaten *vegetables* for us all. But for the wisest of those sitting at the table of the King, a sudden urge arrives, a desire to eat like the Serving King. It, too, is the fruit of *grace* in the chase after the Serving King...

Day 142

THINK...

"Children must be taught how to think, not what to think."
—Margaret Mead

Who are you to pass judgment on the servant of another? It is before
his own master that he stands or falls. And he will be upheld,
for the Lord is able to make him stand.
(Romans 14:4)

The trek after the Serving King would be so much easier if others would simply inform all followers on the specifics of how and where to trek. And fear not, countless are those willing to provide just such advice, particulars of every kind, details remedying the need to *think*. Many are those offering *what to think*. And too many novices in the trek after the Serving King simply fall into line, obediently following the commands of those who have gone before, anxious to lead others down the prescribed and safe path of the Serving King. So they are taught *what to think...*

But the quest after the Serving King rarely follows a well-worn path. Few are those who have walked ahead in precisely the same manner, producing a common path for novices to follow. Instead, every trekker must follow a path built with precision for a party of one. It is the way of the King, the way of the Master. But only those who learn to *think* will learn the art of chasing closely on the heels of the Serving King.

Still, there is a danger for those who learn to *think*, to see the heels of the Serving King just ahead in the path through the grass. Soon comes the temptation to *judge* others who have taken different trails through the grass, different routes, each leading into the distance, too far to see the yet common destination.

But no one chasing after the Serving King answers to the voice of another trekker. Only to the Master does anyone give an accounting for the trail followed. It is the Master who proclaims "...well done, good and faithful servant" (Matthew 25:23). Resist the temptation to run the trail of another. Listen carefully for the voice of the Master. No need to hesitate. Run. The chase is on...

Day 143

FULLY CONVINCED…

"No man ever believes that the Bible means what it says: He is always convinced that it says what he means." —George Bernard Shaw

One person esteems one day as better than another, while another esteems all days alike. Each one should be fully convinced in his own mind.
(Romans 14:5)

Nothing is more distracting on the quest after the Serving King than a *fully convinced* individual hellbent on persuading the rest of the clan of their *fully convinced*. Countless are the hours spent attempting to persuade others of their *fully convinced*. Sadly, the *fully convinced* rarely seem to understand the nature of *fully convinced* and thus make every effort to *fully convince* those who are not *fully convinced*. But *fully convinced* is seldom meant for the public square; rather, it is a custom-designed conviction for a party of one, the *fully convinced*.

More problematic for the *fully convinced* is the temptation to align any *fully convinced* with the teachings of the Serving King in hopes those not *fully convinced* will finally see the wisdom of another's *fully convinced*. Hence, the great temptation to repeatedly be "…convinced that it says what he means." But the Serving King resists every effort to squeeze His teachings into the fancies of the *fully convinced*.

The good news is that *fully convinced* is indeed the intended state of mind for all those chasing along the trail of the Serving King. Nothing is more satisfying in life than to be *fully convinced* that you are chasing along on the exact trail laid out by the Serving King. And therein lies the secret of being *fully convinced*. Those who are genuinely *fully convinced* never sense the urge to *fully convince* anyone. And so comes the secret to a life of great contentment: *simply be fully convinced of the path you are on.*

Expect those less *fully convinced* to make great efforts to dissuade you from the path you tread. It is the sign of the really not *fully convinced*. And you will not be able to persuade them otherwise, precisely because the path you are on was custom-built for a *fully convinced* party of one: you! Chase on…

Day 144

HONOR...

"I would prefer even to fail with honor than win by cheating."
—Sophocles

The one who observes the day, observes it in honor of the Lord. The one who eats, eats in honor of the Lord, since he gives thanks to God, while the one who abstains, abstains in honor of the Lord and gives thanks to God.
(Romans 14:6)

The temptation to *cheat* in the trek after the Serving King is a constant threat, especially in a race filled with guaranteed winners and only a whispering judge, the Spirit of the King, keeping an eye on those running or even stumbling down the trail. The temptation comes only to those watching the trail of another, a course seemingly easier than the one laid out for a party of one. This *day* often seems easier than that *day* and this *eating* easier than *abstaining* or vice versa. Such is the danger of examining the trail of another. And so comes the temptation to *cheat*, to run the course laid out for another.

The temptation only intensifies for those who examine the course laid out for another, discovering the trail over there is genuinely easier than the course laid out for you. And how great the temptation for those who truly understand their status as winner, a guarantee provided by the Serving King, to glide over to a gentler trail. But *honor*, His way of *'being and doing'*, is relentless in its pursuit of those running down the trail of another. *Honor* chides those wooed down the wrong trail.

The *cheater* soon discovers the wisdom behind every course, every trail, custom-designed with one runner in mind. Consequences, not judgment, begin appearing in the life of those on the wrong trail. Hurdles easily cleared by another hinder the path of misguided runners. Abundant life, the fruit lining the course of every trail, eludes the grip of those stumbling down another's course. And great is the frustration of those whose abundant life remains just beyond their fingertips.

Resist the temptation to *cheat*. Run the race with honor. Better to fail with honor than to win while cheating as you chase on...

Day 145

IRRITANT...

"I want to live my life in such a way that when I get out of bed in the morning, the devil says, 'aw shit, he's up!'" —Steve Maraboli

For none of us lives to himself, and none of us dies to himself. For if we live, we live to the Lord, and if we die, we die to the Lord. So then, whether we live or whether we die, we are the Lord's.
(Romans 14:7-8)

Novices to the trek after the Serving King, reclining in the early stages of *grace*, rarely succeed in garnering the attention of the devil, much less irritating him to the point of expletives. As C.S. Lewis made clear in his *Screwtape Letters,* the evil one rarely concerns himself with novices too ingrained in old ways of *'being and doing'* to be of much bother to the cause of darkness. But novices are only novices for a short time as the Serving King unleashes the power of redemption and transformation into every dimension of living or dying, yes, even dying.

Therefore, every novice soon discovers the trek is more about *living* than dying and the life following. Dying will take care of itself. And make no mistake, a life well-lived will indeed catch the attention of the evil one, for in living well the novice makes the greatest impact for the Kingdom of God. Seasoned trekkers are quickly lost in the business of the community of faith, isolated from the old clans, those who most need the touch of the ones chasing after the Serving King. But the novice, not yet rejected by the old clans, wields great influence upon their peers as the redeemed life oozes onto those still entrapped in the old ways of *'being and doing'*. Forgiveness is a glorious moment for the forgiven but rarely noticed by the clan. But the transformed life is quite another thing, impacting everyone who comes in contact.

So comes the challenge to *"...live to the Lord,"* to *be and do* in the present moment in the ways of the King. And rest assured, the evil one will not be pleased, expletives flying from his mouth as you *"...live to the Lord."* Dying will come soon enough. And how glorious to hear him proclaim, "Thank goodness they're gone!" Chase on...

Day 146

LORDSHIP...

"Until the will and the affections are brought under the authority of Christ, we
have not begun to understand, let alone to accept, His lordship."
—Elisabeth Elliot

For to this end Christ died and lived again,
that He might be Lord both of the dead and of the living.
(Romans 14:9)

N ovices to the trek after the Serving King soon discover the vast difference between *Lord* and *Savior*. The latter, an introductory title for new initiates, communicates so very little of the trek yet ahead; instead, it simply provides the courage to stumble onto the steep trail just ahead, to risk falling down, even quitting in those moments of utter exasperation, stunned at His relentless quest to redeem and transform the most broken dimensions of *'being and doing'*. In those moments, the Savior rescues and restores, encouraging the broken to risk just one more step, one more effort to *be and do* in the ways of the Savior. Such is the way of the Savior, rescuing at each and every moment of desperation.

But deep into the quest, deeper than any novice can imagine, comes the challenge to *be* and *do* in ways unfamiliar, threatening, too intimidating for the average novice to press on farther into the steepest grades. And in that moment, the *Lord* appears, mandating just one more step, a bit farther up the trail, crawling if need be, even to the point of *death*. This is no mere *Savior* content to rescue the perishing, to pour balm on the wounds of the trail. This is King of Kings, Lord of Lords. He is never content to merely save, to carry the broken into the throne room of the King. No, He is a Savior of another kind, one who means to be *Lord*, even when the novice trembles in fear before the face of death.

But this Lord waits patiently "...until the will and affections are brought under the authority of Christ," the Lord. He will only be Lord for those who beckon Him to take the throne to be Lord. And He is patient, willing to wait, content to be Savior until the moment of Lordship arrives. Chase on...

Day 147

PROXIMITY...

"We should not judge people by their peak of excellence; but by the distance they have traveled from the point where they started."
—Harriet Ward Beecher

Why do you pass judgment on your brother? Or you, why do you despise your brother? For we will all stand before the judgment seat of God; for it is written,
"As I live, says the Lord, every knee shall bow to Me,
and every tongue shall confess to God."
(Romans 14:10-11)

Proximity creates an illusion. And illusions are always problematic in the trek after the Serving King. Co-trekkers, those in *proximity*, create an urge, rising up from deep within, irresistible at times, to *judge* other trekkers, especially the weak and wounded, those whose chasing skills lack your grace, excellence and refinement. And so arrives the *illusion*, the grand misunderstanding, that all trekkers *start from the same place.* They do not. Some have come farther than you can imagine. Some, just steps away from their beginning place. Nor do all trekkers have the same abilities, the same inner being, or even the same flesh. All are uniquely wounded by sin, no two sinners alike, no two trekkers on similar trails, no two pilgrims progressing in an identical manner. Such is only the *illusion of proximity.*

So comes the warning to stop judging those in *proximity.* Judging is but a fool's game, an activity for novices soon forbidden to all who would continue on to the deepest points in the trek after the Serving King. And the *foolish judge*, still early in the quest, riding the Spirit's wave to a *peak of excellence*, foolishly thinks she has walked to this peak, oblivious to the Spirit who carried her. But this *peak of excellence* in the quest after the Serving King is but one in a long line of peaks throughout a lifetime, all leading to the presence of the King.

The *illusion* of the peak disappears in the presence of the King, reality crashing in on all making their way to the throne room of the King. The standard, no more and no less than the Serving King Himself, incredibly high, renders all efforts mere folly, fools stumbling in the dark, peaks nothing more than hills. There will be no illusion of judging here, only awe at the mountain peak of His throne. The chase is close to home...

Day 148

ACCOUNTING...

"Facts are facts and will not disappear on account of your likes."
—Jawaharlal Nehru

So then each of us will give an account of himself to God.
(Romans 14:12)

Novices love *grace*, not the *grace* of the NT, but non-redemptive *grace*, the *get-out-of-jail* grace, the never give "...an account of himself to God" kind of grace requiring no transformation in the life of those chasing after the Serving King. But such is not the *grace of redemption*. The *grace of redemption* charges into the life of everyone chasing after the Serving King. It empowers as it transforms bringing about profound changes, redeeming heart, mind, body, and soul. Redemptive grace is comprehensive, tackling every facet of what it means to be human, what it means to be a Christ follower, what it means to chase God into the highest realms. It is *redemptive grace* that knows an accounting before God awaits. God expects an accounting from everyone. It is God's way.

But the *grace of redemption* fears no accounting before God, not because there has been perfect success, but, rather, because *redemptive grace* stands in the shadows of the Serving King. It is He who will provide all righteousness as each God-chaser finally stands in the presence of God. Nonetheless, each God-chaser delights in the authentic transformations that have occurred. Hence, the accounting is not an event to be feared but, instead, celebrated. The 'fact' is that God has done so much! God has transformed the horribly broken and brought about redemption and transformation.

Freed by the *redemptive grace* of God, judgment toward others flees. Judgment knows transformation and freedom were created by God, liberating the enslaved from the sin that so easily entangles. Now liberated, the God-chaser waits patiently for the liberation in others equally committed to chasing after the Serving King. The day is soon coming when they too will know the redemptive power of transformation. The day of accounting comes soon enough. In the meantime, patience as the chase continues...

Day 149

HINDRANCE...

"We stumble and fall constantly even when we are most enlightened. But when we are in true spiritual darkness, we do not even know that we have fallen."
—Thomas Merton

Therefore let us not pass judgment on one another any longer, but rather decide never to put a stumbling block or hindrance in the way of a brother.
(Romans 14:13)

Enlightenment, genuinely understanding His way of 'being and doing', sheds tremendous light on the path ahead. Unfortunately, enlightenment is always personal, revelation for one. It is custom-built for one, you, even if another has been given the same light. But the many, simply by comparing notes, begin to assume everyone must receive the same revelation, and not only revelation, but application as well. So arrives the grand temptation to "...put a stumbling block or hinderance in the way of a brother." It is the result of comparing light, and then assuming everyone must have received the same light.

But such is not the way of the Serving King. Revelation rarely goes forth in a universal manner but, rather, one individual at a time, step by step, piece by piece. Those with additional pieces are often tempted to insist everyone else abide by the piece that God has provided for them, but such is not the case. Revelation custom-built for you is rarely helpful to someone else; instead, it's simply a road-block hindering their trek deeper into the quest after the Serving King.

Conversely, revelation provided to and for you has been extremely helpful in moving you deeper into the quest, hence, your temptation to offer it to others. But today is not the day for their enlightenment. God has provided lessons better suited for their unique quest. Resist the temptation to insist that others see what you see, understand what you understand. Instead, simply acknowledge that God is at work in the unique way that God is always at work in those chasing after the Serving King. And yes, be not surprised when your obedience to the revelation you have received matches the obedience of others equally committed to the chase. One person's revelation is another's roadblock. Refrain from placing roadblocks as you chase on...

Day 150

CRACKED EGGS...

"A true friend is someone who thinks that you are a good egg even though he knows that you are slightly cracked." —Bernard Meltzer

I know and am persuaded in the Lord Jesus that nothing is unclean in itself, but it is unclean for anyone who thinks it unclean. For if your brother is grieved by what you eat, you are no longer walking in love. By what you eat, do not destroy the one for whom Christ died. (Romans 14:14-15)

N ovices often assume every moment of personal revelation, insights into the particulars of the trail ahead, are meant for every trekker tracking after the Serving King. So the temptation to play the mailman, informing others, those *cracked eggs* traveling nearby, of the trail intended by the Serving King. The problem, of course, is no two *cracked eggs* are cracked in exactly the same manner. Thus, every trail is custom-built for the unique *crackedness* of each egg on the journey.

Few equally understand the precision with which every trail is custom-designed down to the tiniest detail, even the food eaten along the trail. The *crackedness* of each egg mandates the need for different trails loaded with different foods, custom diets designed for the unique *crackedness of each egg*. Hence, what is *clean* for one *cracked egg* will be unclean for another. And the only way to distinguish clean from unclean is the personal instruction of the Serving King.

Thankfully, every cracked egg begins to realize every egg, including self, has a crack or two. Some cracks are big, some are small, some are straight, some are jagged, but in the end, every egg is cracked in one way or another. And so, the church is never anything more than the gathering of *cracked eggs* who have learned to love each others *good eggness* in spite of the glaring cracks.

Fortunately, *cracks* are never the last word. The Serving King is in the business of repairing *cracked eggs*. And the sooner each *cracked egg* follows the customized diet and trail behind the Serving King, the sooner the *cracks* disappear. But understand, there are more cracks below the surface. There is yet much repair work to be done in the chase...

Day 151

NOTHING TO TALK ABOUT...

"I often regret that I have spoken; never that I have been silent."
—Publilius Syrus

So do not let what you regard as good be spoken of as evil.
For the kingdom of God is not a matter of eating and drinking
but of righteousness and peace and joy in the Holy Spirit.
(Romans 14:16-18)

People talk. And then they talk some more. And if there is any air left in the room, they talk even more. Talking is the signature of the human condition, proof of their existence, part of the human DNA. Sadly, rarely is their talking void of evaluation. Thus, the path of the Serving King is abuzz with conversation as those chasing after the Serving King entertain themselves with conversation. Gossip in all of its glory. The novice trekker too often joins the conversation, thinking critique a proper form of communication, an appropriate entertainment for those chasing after the Serving King in the close company of the many. So the many march along in the hum of conversation: gossip, by another name.

Thus comes the expectation for a command of silence, a cessation of all *people talk*, a mandate to speak no evil, to avoid evaluations of all kinds. But it does not come. Instead, an unanticipated challenge to cease and desist from all activity generating something to talk about. Missing is the command to *be silent!* In its place is the challenge to *give them nothing to talk about*.

The cease and desist challenge makes perfect sense in regards to *inappropriate activity, evil,* but this is no challenge to stop behaving badly; rather, it's a shocking challenge to disengage from activity *"...you regard as good."* You will be tempted to challenge the Serving King, to carry on with *good* behavior, to exercise liberty, to set an example of *goodness* for the unenlightened. But the Serving King will have none of that. This is not about teaching others the *good* way to behave. This is about being kind and gentle toward those who have not yet been exposed to the *good* custom-built for you. The Serving King will introduce them to the *good* of your path soon enough. But that is never your concern. Be faithful in giving them *nothing to talk about* as you chase on...

Day 152

THE GREASED PIG...

"Peace is not absence of conflict, it is the ability to handle conflict by peaceful means." —Ronald Reagan

So then let us pursue what makes for peace and for mutual upbuilding.
(Romans 14:19)

Peace is illusive, and the quest to find it exhausting; nonetheless, the call of the Serving King to pursue it is clear, unmistakeable. And His peace is a peace of a special kind, not the mundane *lack of conflict* but *mutual upbuilding*, enriching the life of all those blessed by peace. This is the distinctive nature of the peace to be pursued. But you will be tempted to settle for a mere lack of conflict, the peace the world too often offers, a peace easily afforded to those willing and wanting to live in isolation away from the demands of the many. Still the Serving King is clear in His intention, mandating all those chasing after Him to pursue a higher ground, a ground amongst the many working in unity for the edification of all.

But His peace is slippery in the community of the many, the proverbial *greased pig*, nearly impossible to seize as the many clamor for *"have it your way."* You will pursue it, occasionally corner it, leap for it, even grab it from time to time, but holding onto it is nearly impossible. Self-interest, the antithesis of peace, the *grease on the pig*, oozes out from the many, rendering peace illusive at all times, constantly on the move, a moving target of the worst kind.

Still, trek after the Serving King is never ultimately about catching the illusive *greased pig* but, rather, the pursuit of peace, His peace. And in those rare moments when those chasing after the Serving King seize His way of *'being and doing'*, the illusive *greased pig* suddenly appears, easily corralled, calm and pleased to abide in the company of the many. But the *greased pig* startles easily at the first signs of self-interest, the old way of *'being and doing'*, ever lurking just below the surface of those chasing after the Serving King...

Day 153

FOOD WARS...

"Food, in the end, in our own tradition, is something holy. It's not about nutrients and calories. It's about sharing. It's about honesty. It's about identity." —Louise Fresco

Do not, for the sake of food, destroy the work of God. Everything is indeed clean, but it is wrong for anyone to make another stumble by what he eats. It is good not to eat meat or drink wine or do anything that causes your brother to stumble.
(Romans 14:20-21)

Novice trekkers, too well-schooled in the old ways of *'being and doing'* to simply abandon them, often travel along the trail of the Serving King with sword in hand, ready to fight in the final gladiatorial conquest, the battle of ideas. And far too often the battle rages over the mundane, the insignificant, the ultimately meaningless affairs of personal lifestyle in the quest after the Serving King. And so, the *food wars* often begin, creating casualties of all ages, wounded saints strewn in the worship plaza.

And for all their decrying of war, humans are quick to engage, fighting over the mundane as though it maintained any real significance in the Kingdom of God. *Food wars* rage on all in the name of service to the King. But the King has no interest in *food wars,* nor clothing wars, nor styles of worship wars, not any of the vast array of personal lifestyle choices mandated by the infection of sin.

Nonetheless, there are those in the community of faith whose trail has been designed especially for them, crippled by the infection of sin, and thereby limited in what can be consumed, what can be experienced. Theirs is a restricted walk in the land of the free. Thus the Serving King's command to trod gently amongst those so restricted amidst the free.

Many are those wounded by the freedoms of another. So the command to exercise freedom with your brothers and sisters in mind. This is no hypocrisy, a make-pretend world where authenticity should reign. No, this is a world where compassion and concern for the *less free* reigns in the behavior of the redeemed. Be of good cheer. There will be many days to live in your freedom, days when your brothers and sisters are safely tucked away. Chase on in the gentle ways of compassion...

Day 154

DINE WITH THE KING...

"They that approve a private opinion, call it opinion; but they that dislike it, heresy; and yet heresy signifies no more than private opinion."
—Thomas Hobbs

The faith that you have, keep between yourself and God. Blessed is the one who has no reason to pass judgment on himself for what he approves.
(Romans 14:22)

The trek after the Serving King is filled with *revelation,* insight into His ways of *'being and doing',* personalized for those remaining within hearing distance of the Pathfinder. And once heard, the temptation to share the *Good News* can be overwhelming at times, creating an irresistible urge to share the harvest with other starving peasants along the way. But you must resist, *"...the faith that you have, keep between yourself and God."* But some, too immature in the faith to resist the urge, thinking such *Good News* a blessing intended for all, simply cannot resist. And so, the *food wars* erupt with each new trekker joining the feast with the Serving King.

But life in community often demands difficult menu decisions complicated by the vast number of trekkers dining at the table with the Serving King. And no two trekkers, each diseased uniquely by the infection of sin, ever require exactly the same menu; hence, the battles flare over and over again as the easily offended stake their ground, remaining resistant to dining at the table with any unacceptable menu item. So the proliferation of menus arise as trekkers begin to gather at tables of the like-minded.

But there is a guest at every table, laughing and enjoying the company of the like-minded, robustly eating all that is set before Him as He saunters from table to table. He has no reason to *pass judgment on Himself for what He approves,* no reason to pass on any delectable tidbit placed before Him. Instead, He casually dines with each table of the infected. Such are the ways of the Serving King.

There is coming a grand banquet with the King but not today. And yes, at that final banquet, foods of all kinds will appear, and there will be no restrictions at the banquet of the King. And best of all, you can eat them all as you chase on...

Day 155

THE FOOL'S BANQUET...

*"A lot of people out there pay good lip service to the idea of personal freedom...
right up to the point that someone tries to do something that they don't
personally approve of." —Neal Boortz*

*But whoever has doubts is condemned if he eats, because the eating is not
from faith. For whatever does not proceed from faith is sin.
(Romans 14:23)*

K nowledge of the banquet to come often tempts those chasing after the
Serving King to eat prematurely, to feast on the vast array of foods waiting
at the banquet of the King, and more so as others feast so freely on delicious forbidden tidbits. The novice, still not persuaded every trail custom-built, struggles
to stay the course while others feast freely on foods left along the way by the
Serving King. Longing for *revelation* of another kind, the trek becomes exceed-
ingly difficult while distracted by the trek of another.

Some, seeing the many eat free from concern of any kind, consider abandoning the precision trail of the Serving King and following another's trail. The
aromas along another's trail wafting in the breeze, too enticing to ignore, too
distracting to remain on the heels of the Serving King. And so, their wandering
begins along the trail of another, the entryway into the wilderness, a journey to
nowhere at the *fool's banquet.*

The *fool*, having heard the voice of the Serving King, a warning to stay the
course, to resist the trail of another, abandons the life of faith, too enticed by
another's life of faith. Thus, the fool crawls into the life of *grace*, meandering
along the trail of another, leaving the life of faith behind. But the life of *grace*
comes with consequences, painful at times, robbing the woeful trekker of the
intended abundant life. It is the life of sin, *"...for whatever does not proceed
from faith is sin."*

But there is yet *Good News* for those dining at the *fool's banquet.* The trail
of the Serving King is ever-present awaiting your return. The life of sin has no
power over you other than the power you give it. While others continue to eat,
push the plate away, rise from the table, and return to the banquet prepared
just for you. Chase on...

Day 156

OBLIGATIONS...

"The weak can never forgive. Forgiveness is the attribute of the strong."
—Mahatma Ghandi

We who are strong have an obligation to bear with the failings of the weak,
and not to please ourselves.
(Romans 15:1)

Peace which comprehensively edifies the heaviest of the lofty goals of the Serving King for the community of the many is rarely ushered in by the weak, too busy exercising their newly-bestowed freedom in ways of self-interest. Still, the exercise of freedom in following the Serving King soon produces a strength known only to those whose stamina allows them to follow on the heels of the Serving King into the deepest realms of the quest. But strength always comes with an *obligation* to carry the *failings of the weak,* those unable to climb the steepest grades of the quest.

The *weak,* too anemic to battle the old ways of *'being and doing'*, surrender to the *old-self* raging within demanding obedience to self-interest liberated by freedoms made accessible by the Serving King. But the freedoms of another irritate and agitate those in the earliest stages of freedom yet consumed with *pleasing ourselves.*

So comes the challenge to the *strong*, those most able to battle the desire to *please ourselves:* to hold the beast of *self-interest* in check while in the company of the *weak.* But resisting the urge to flee from the *weaklings*, tiresome as they can be, can be overwhelming at times. But the trail of the Serving King always leads back to the community of the many, the gathering of weaklings too enthralled in the wooing of *self-interest* to live in peace, a peace which edifies the many. But it is only in the gathering of the many that the *strong* find opportunity to abandon the lure of isolation to join the Serving King in ministering to the clan of *weaklings.*

You will be tempted to abandon the *obligation* to carry the weaklings, to live in the community of the many, to join the Serving King in exercising *grace.* But resist, you must, if you are to follow the Serving King into realms deep. The chase continues...

Day 157

THE STOOP...

*"A man is called selfish not for pursuing his own good,
but for neglecting his neighbor's." —Richard Whately*

Let each of us please his neighbor for his good, to build him up.
(Romans 15:2)

Neighbors, followers of the Serving King or not, are difficult to *please*. Plain and simple. Nonetheless, pleasing them would be so much easier, if the exhortation were to simply *please* them, to make them happy or content. But the Serving King is rarely satisfied with so singular and simple a task; instead, mandating a much tougher standard, a modus operandi ever evolving into particulars uniquely suited for each independent neighbor, specifics with only the *good* in mind. And neighbors are rarely interested in what is *good for them,* rather, simply what pleases them, assuming the two to be synonymous, which, of course, they are not. The challenge to *please* in a specific manner, *for his good, to build him up,* is exceeding difficult in a world in which *for his good*, is too often perceived by neighbor as unpleasant and distasteful.

And *moderns* work exceptionally hard at ignoring neighbors and being ignored, building private castles equipped with *slip in, slip out* technologies dismantling the need for even cursory greetings, the stepping stones of authentic relationship. Without authentic relationship, neighbors are ill-equipped to provide what is *good* for each other. And so, silence reigns.

Still, the Serving King rarely makes provision for chasing alone for extended periods; instead, insisting on life in community, even the building of neighborly stoops, inviting vestibules awaiting conversations of all kinds, even authentic conversations between neighbors threatening to actually become friends, people who *know* each other.

Rest assured, if you build it, this old-fashioned stoop, they will come, neighbors of all kinds, chasing after the Serving King, led by Him to join you for a moment or two of authentic conversation. And be prepared, for when they *know* you, they will indeed seek to please you in the ways of the Serving King, providing what is *good, to build you up* in the ways of the Serving King. Chase on...

Day 158

UPBRAID...

*"Behold, I am become a reproach to thy holy name, by serving any ambition
and the sins of others; which though I did by the persuasion of other men, yet
my own conscience did cheek and upbraid me in it."*
—William Laud

*For Christ did not please Himself, but as it is written,
"The reproaches of those who reproached you fell on Me."
(Romans 15:3)*

The *good for neighbor* is often costly, more costly than you will care to bear. It can be unpleasant, contrary to what pleases self, even for the Christ. Even the Serving King flinched at the self-sacrifice necessary for the *good for neighbor.* Loving your neighbor, genuinely desiring what is best for them, comes late in the chase after the Serving King, just as the final payment came late in the life of the Serving King.

Still, His way of *'being and doing'* has taken root deep within, refusing to sit quietly at the foot of opportunity, the moment of self-sacrifice for the sake of neighbor. Self-interest, seeing the cost, rises to the surface, attempting to dissuade you from the path of self-sacrifice. Self-interest challenges you to please yourself and forget this path of sacrificial love for others. Self preservation threatens your final development into a child of the Serving King.

But His way of *'being and doing'* will indeed *"...check and upbraid me in it,"* calling self-interest to stand down, to surrender to that which is *good for neighbor.* This is a new way of *being and doing,* the late arriving fruit in the chase after the Serving King. His way is becoming your way. Fear not as He calls you to a new way of *'being and doing."*

Take no offense as He upbraids you, challenges you to rise above self-interest, to step into the reproach intended for neighbor. It is the way of the Serving King. And, in that moment, you enter the final stages of the chase after the Serving King. Expect little company as you head into the deepest realms of the quest. Few are those willing to sacrifice self-interest for the sake of the Kingdom. But you are amongst the few, those willing to endure the *upbraid* of the King. The chase begins in earnest now...

Day 159

READ AHEAD…

"Endurance is not just the ability to bear a hard thing,
but to turn it into glory." —William Barclay

For whatever was written in former days was written for our instruction,
that through endurance and through the encouragement of the
Scriptures we might have hope.
(Romans 15:4)

Suffering, of any kind, is never pleasant, but unexpected suffering is often unbearable, especially for novices expecting pleasantries along the trail of the Serving King. Some, ignoring the call to *read ahead*, to preview what *was written for our instruction*, run enthusiastically down the trail, ignoring the steepening grade, confident natural ability will carry them along the way. Unprepared, failing to *read ahead*, the novice soon stumbles as the first pangs of suffering arrive, shocking the ill-prepared into the painful reality of chasing after the Serving King. Confused and bewildered, but remembering the earlier challenge to *read ahead*, the novice often turns to the *written for our instruction* just in the nick of time. Rarely are the ill-prepared able to "…bear a hard thing, but turn it into glory."

But there are those few, the well-prepared, those who *read ahead*, ready to embrace the consequences of chasing after the Serving King. They also soon encounter the necessary pangs of chasing deepest into the trail of the Serving King, but having *read ahead*, the expected pangs arrive on schedule, just as those who wrote in *former days* predicted. The wisdom of previous trekkers prepares and equips those who *read ahead* for all that is about to come. Preparing those to follow is the very purpose of those who wrote *in former days*.

It is they who *read ahead* who are prepared to not only "…bear a hard thing, but turn it into glory." It is the way of the Serving King; seeing the cross before Him, He embraced it to the glory of God. He, too, *read ahead*, knowing all that was to come. Like Him, *read ahead* as far as you can, beyond the suffering to be endured. There is a glorious end to the tale of your trek after the Serving King. Go ahead, read ahead, and then chase on into the glorious future that is waiting…

Day 160

SYMPHONY...

"Harmony makes small things grow, lack of it makes great things decay."
—Sallust

*May the God of endurance and encouragement grant you to live
in such harmony with one another, in accord with Christ Jesus.
(Romans 15:5)*

Harmony is illusive, more illusive yet in the gathering of the elect, those destined to share in the greatness of the Kingdom of God. The problem, unexpectedly, is revelation, personal and intimate, customer built for every God-chaser. God, more intimately in tune with us than we could ever imagine, custom builds a journey for each of us. Unfortunately, insecure in our ability to hear and follow the Serving King, friction appears as God-chasers cross paths, needing and wanting assurances from others chasing after the Serving King. Assurances not forthcoming, the tension builds as co-journeyers attempt to match experiences, paths, and destinations.

But harmony in the Kingdom of God requires no such homogenization of experiences, paths, and destinations; instead, a harmonizing of following the trail of the Serving King. Those on the trail of the Serving King soon discover divergent paths, crisscrossing here and there, but often separate and diverse, each ending at the throne of the King. Only at the throne of the King do God-chasers experience a blessed harmony of the purest kind.

Only then do they discover the symphony filled with instruments of every kind, from trails so utterly diverse all playing in unison, each with its unique sound, together, music worthy of worship and praise. This is the harmony of the Serving King, the symphony worthy of the Father, an overpowering orchestra of praise, to the glory of the Serving King. So arrive those who all along have been "...in accord with Jesus Christ." Only in the presence of every 'other' does the harmony of those chasing the Serving King rise to the heavens. This is the crescendo of the people of God as they finally arrive, finely tuned, each playing precisely the music the Serving King intended all along. So the symphony of the many harmoniously finds greatness. Chase on...

Day 161

How Did You Get In Here...

"I had crossed the line. I was free; but there was no one to welcome me to the
land of freedom. I was a stranger in a strange land."
—Harriet Tubman

...that together you may with one voice glorify the God and Father
of our Lord Jesus Christ. Therefore welcome one another
as Christ has welcomed you, for the glory of God.
(Romans 15:6-7)

The story is often told of the God-chaser who died and found himself gloriously transformed into his heavenly home. Saint Peter greeted him at the
gate, graciously offering to show him around. Together, they strolled the halls of
the heavenly realm, pausing at every door to peek inside as each group gathered
in praise and worship. Upon approaching the door ahead, Peter cautioned him,
"Be quiet as you pass, they are gathered here. They think they are the only ones
here." Fill in your favorite group.

Sadly, God-chasers often have the sense of 'rightness', frequently to the
exclusion of everyone else. But entrance into the Kingdom of heaven has never
been a matter of right thinking, rather, faith: a simple response of trust to that
which God has made known. Faith is always intimate and personal. Faith simply
responds to whatever God makes known. It is the way of Abraham and all who
would follow after him.

You will be surprised as well by those who have made it to the party before
you and those who will join the party after you. You will be be tempted to ask,
"How did you get in here?" Resist the temptation. Jesus has provided for people
of all nations to arrive at the party, the grand celebration of faith, each with a
custom-built understanding of how God would have faith to express itself.

But this is a strange new land for everyone, filled with people of every kind,
each uniquely related to the Serving King. Simply delight in their arrival. Waste
no time trying to understand how they arrived. Faith is the key all must have,
if they are to arrive in the strange new land. Make sure no one enters alone.
Welcome everyone as they, like you, have simply chased on...

Day 162

SINGING IN THE SHOWER...

"The woods would be quiet if no bird sang but the one that sang best."
—*Henry Van Dyke*

For I tell you that Christ became a servant to the circumcised to show God's truthfulness, in order to confirm the promises given to the patriarchs, and in order that the Gentiles might glorify God for His mercy. As it is written, "Therefore I will praise you among the Gentiles, and sing to Your name."
(Romans 15:8-9)

Showers are often filled with less than perfect pitch, for in the sanctuary of the shower no one critiques, no one ridicules, no one seems to notice, especially the singer. So the sanctuary of the shower often reverberates the glory of God as the pitter-patter of running water liberates the singer, free to *sing Your name,* delivered from all concern from those who mandate *perfect pitch,* especially the singer. The shower ushers in the sanctuary of mercy, grace toward all imperfections in those who sing. Sadly, once the shower ceases, too often all singing cascades down the drain, chasing the water to nowhere, a place free from ears that can hear.

But the birds have much to teach us about singing praises of God. The woods are never silent, filled instead with the cacophony of off-key beasts of the air, each singing with no concern for perfect pitch, or even pleasant pitch. Their only concern is to sing gloriously for their Creator. And so, the weakest and strongest, pleasant and unpleasant, elegant and mundane, join in unison proclaiming the majesty of the Creator.

But those chasing after the Serving King often sing only when all is right, perfect pitch. Alas, the trek after the Serving King is too exhausting for perfect pitch. No one, except the Son, has perfect pitch. Yet, the King delights in the pitch of all those on the trail of His Son.

And when the woods go silent, the Gentiles never hear His name, never experience the glorious praise of those who trek after the Serving King. Better to sing off-key than to never sing at all. Go ahead, step out of the shower, sing with gusto. And be not surprised when others sing off-key right along with you, all to the glory of the King. Sing on...

Day 163

BETTER LATE THAN NEVER...

"Ah, Nothing is too late, till the tired heart shall cease to palpitate."
—Henry Wadsworth Longfellow

And again it is said, "Rejoice, O Gentiles, with His people." And again, "Praise the Lord, all you Gentiles, and let all the peoples extol Him."
(Romans 15:10-11)

The many, far into realms too deep, fear the Serving King has no place for them on His quest toward redemption, no way to extend His grace into the depths of despair. Within the depths of despair, a dread overwhelms as the old ways of *'being and doing'* sing an old, familiar song, a song known too well by the many, the urge to sing old tunes raging, forbidding the words of a new song from ever finding a home in the old ways of *'being and doing'*. And so, the despair overwhelms as old songs continue to play in the heart and mind of those in realms too deep. The chorus rings in the canyons of despair overpowering those who long for a new song, a new way of *'being and doing'*.

But the Serving King can indeed extend His voice into the abyss, realms too deep. He whispers words of praise into the ears of those long enslaved to songs of old. But old songs lie in their claim to supremacy. It is but a bluff, an intimidation, an idle threat, void of the necessary power to squelch the power of praise in the *tired heart*. Rage as they may, old songs can do nothing to hinder the words of praise as they flow from the ear to the heart. And any *tired heart,* old and feeble, can still whisper the words of praise, the words of the Serving King. Once whispered, praise leaps to the rescue of the feeblest heart, restoring power and vitality, energy to the exhausted. The fading heart responds, whispering anew, repeating the *praise* of the Serving King.

So a new song slowly emerges as the old tunes surrender to *praise*. The few courageous enough to whisper praise in realms too deep, soon discover it is never too late to join *His people* in a chorus of praise as together you chase on...

Day 164

LITTLE OPPORTUNITY...

"If people perceive themselves as having very little opportunities to be fulfilled, then it cheapens their life and outlook. The solution is to reverse it; make sure they know opportunities abound." —Michael Lee Chin

And again Isaiah says, "The root of Jesse will come, even He who arises to rule the Gentiles; in Him will the Gentiles hope." May the God of hope fill you with all joy and peace in believing, so that by the power of the Holy Spirit you may abound in hope.
(Romans 15:12-13)

Those long lost in realms too deep often lose *hope*, fearful too many opportunities have passed for a return to the trail home, the path of the Serving King. But the Serving King knows no limits, no forest too thick, no desert too dry, no sea too violent, no heart too feeble. He is the *root* that has come, the path in the forest, the living water in the desert, the calm in the roughest sea, the power to revive the weakest heart. Tragically, those long lost in realms too deep often "...perceive themselves as having *little opportunity*."

But *little opportunity* is all that is needed for those who sense the *root of Jesse*, the footprint of the Serving King, the trace of His scent, the trail of His path. Much is not needed to begin the trek after the Serving King. *Little opportunity* is all that is needed. Just enough hope to turn in the right direction, to take the first step home, to begin the trek after the Serving King. Once the trek begins, He is faithful to send His Spirit thriving with power for even the weakest, even those most feeble on the trail after the Serving King. The journey home unfolds one modest step at a time.

So hope abounds in those who have encountered the power of *little opportunity*, the *root of Jesse*, the ruler of the Gentiles. But this is no mere change of spirit in those forever lost in realms too deep; no, this is the arrival of the power to go home, to *abound in hope*, to see the next step, to follow the footsteps of the Serving King on the path homeward from realms too deep. And those on the trail of the Serving King soon discover the power of walking in the right direction, homeward bound, from realms too deep. The power of hope has arrived. Chase on...

Day 165

CLARITY OF INSTRUCTION...

"We teach best by how we live life; who we are instructs with absolute clarity."
—Bryant McGill

I myself am satisfied about you, my brothers, that you yourselves are full of goodness, filled with all knowledge and able to instruct one another.
(Romans 15:14)

You would think those *full of goodness, filled with all knowledge*, would have no need of further instruction, especially from *one another*. Shocking to discover Paul's suggestion, only those in the maturity of faith, *full of goodness, filled with all knowledge*, ones chasing after the Serving King are ready to finally instruct one another. It is the final stage, the culmination of years of learning.

But this final instruction is far less verbal than one anticipates; instead, instruction with *absolute clarity* is rarely with words. To the contrary, words often obstruct and confuse, get in the way of *clarity of instruction*. All that can be said, has been said, clears the way for this final *clarity of instruction*. Clarity arrives only in incarnation, in the *Word became flesh and dwelt among us* (John 1:14). Only in *fleshing out* words does instruction find its final moments of clarity. Only as His words become our flesh does the final stage of *clarity of instruction* finally arrive, only in *being* and finally *doing*.

So this final stage of *clarity of instruction* is taught best by "...how we live," as the trek after the Serving King is lived out in the day-to-day turmoil of everyday life. There is no need of instruction by mouth in this final stage. No need for verbalization. Only by walking in the trek itself can those in the final stages *instruct one another*.

But you will be tempted to talk some more, to instruct with words, to remain in the safety of mere conversation, to avoid the *clarity of instruction* through incarnation. Rare are those who finally begin to *instruct one another* through a life well-lived. The time has come to stop talking, to finally engage in His ways of *'being and doing'*. You have arrived at the destination *grace* has been bringing you all along. Time to *be and do* in the ways of the King as you chase on...

Day 166

BEYOND GOOD INTENTIONS...

"What one does is what counts. Not what one had the intention of doing."
—*Pablo Picasso*

*But on some points I have written to you very boldly by way of reminder,
because of the grace given me by God to be a minister of Christ Jesus to the
Gentiles in the priestly service of the gospel of God, so that the offering of the
Gentiles may be acceptable, sanctified by the Holy Spirit.*
(Romans 15:15-16)

Many, encouraged by the trek of those whose *clarity of instruction* shines like a beacon on a hill in the darkest of nights, begin the trek after the Serving King intending to march toward that beacon. Armed with good intentions, exuberance oozing from within, the many charge into the quest, confident the hill well within walking distance; and, indeed it is, but not nearly so close as the novice imagines.

But the trek after the Serving King is a long one, longer than the most seasoned vets expected, burning every ounce of exuberance, rendering even the hardiest of trekkers sluggards as the grade steepens toward the beacon on the hill. And seasoned veterans, knowing the trail ahead, *boldly remind* you of the commitment to succeed, to carry on regardless of cost. And so, they cheer for your success, *boldly reminding* you of the call of the Serving King. Nonetheless, the challenge to conquer the hill requires far more than mere good intentions, more than the bold reminders and encouragement from veterans of previous treks, more than you are capable of having finally arrived at the moment of *sanctification*. You have come as far as you are able. Well done. But you have not finished, have not become able to provide *clarity of instruction*.

There is still trail un-trekked, journeys yet unexperienced, farther to go for those desiring *clarity of instruction,* a life reflecting the glory of His ways of *'being and doing'*. But this is the domain of the Spirit, requiring a *sanctifying* made possible in Him, a freedom and release from the old ways of *'being and doing'* only He can provide. *Sanctification* is the deathblow to the carnal still residing in your *being* and consequent *doing*. Only He can *sanctify*. And so He does. Walk on. There is coming a strength you could not have imagined as you chase on...

172

Day 167

PROUD OF MY WORK...

"It's not about working anymore, its about doing work I can be proud of."
—Paul Walker

In Christ Jesus, then, I have reason to be proud of my work for God.
(Romans 15:17)

Pride often takes a beating in the Kingdom of God and, most of the time, for good reason. Too often *pride* is an unhealthy boasting easily discerned by others, creating emotional barriers only crossed with great difficulty. Pride of this kind hinders authentic community. It is rooted in self rather than Serving King.

But there is a *pride of another kind* rising up out of authentic fellowship with the Serving King. Gone are the days of attempting to work your way into the Kingdom of God. In its place a rich relationship with Jesus, the foundation of all righteousness before God. Still, there is an unexpected fruit in this intimate relationship, an intense desire to *work* for Him who loves you so deeply prior to any working at all on your part.

Thus, you are able to join Paul Walter in proclaiming, "It's not about the work anymore..." But finally, after all this time, there arrives a deep desire to work for the Serving King. And not just any work, but work you will be proud of, work He will be proud of. It is the work of ministry, engaging others in the challenge to finally begin chasing after the Serving King.

It is the warmest of heartfelt moments as you see the lives of others so radically impacted by the abiding presence of the Serving King. Like yourself, the presence of Jesus has brought drastic changes. Lives once broken and hopeless, now running down the trail after the Serving King, overjoyed by the *sanctification* He has brought to so many. No longer chasing on alone, the many now run beside you, laughing, beaming with joy, lives radically transformed by the presence of the Serving King. No, it is no longer about working more, it is about the work you can be proud of, the joy of celebrating new life with those whom God has transformed through your chase after the Serving King. Chase on, there is more joy yet ahead...

Day 168

ROAD BUILDING...

"Sometimes we get caught up in trying to glorify God by praising what He can do and we lose sight of the practical point of what He actually does do."
—Dallas Willard

For I will not venture to speak of anything except what Christ has accomplished through me to bring the Gentiles to obedience—by word and deed, by the power of signs and wonders, by the power of the Spirit of God— so that from Jerusalem and all the way around to Illyricum I have fulfilled the ministry of the gospel of Christ.
(Romans 15:18-19)

It is a strange moment when the trek after the Serving King becomes produc-tive, not for your quest but for the quest of another, a very unfamiliar other. Ultimately, every quest after the Serving King turns toward those unconnected, disobedient travelers, wayward souls, lost in a landscape with few roads home. So every trek builds roads for wayward travelers to find their way home. You are now a road builder.

And rarely does the *road home* simply appear; instead, it is painstakingly built by those chasing after the Serving King, establishing the path, clearing the way, step by step, piece by piece, *words and deeds* carefully laid down by road builders committed to leading others home. You will be tempted to ignore the painstaking process of building roads, brick by brick, relying instead on the *signs and wonders by the power of the Spirit of God* to lay the bricks on the road home. But road building is a multifaceted endeavor requiring helping hands from many lands, workers all empowered by the abiding presence of the Holy Spirit.

So comes the temptation to *glorify God by praising what He can do* rather than laying bricks of *word and deed,* His ways of *'being and doing'.* But be of good cheer, this road is completed, not by your efforts alone, or the efforts of your co-workers, rather by the *power of signs and wonders* provided by the Spirit of God. The journey home can only be completed by Him, the Miracle Worker, the One who transforms body and spirit into receptacles of the Holy Spirit.

Your task is to simply build the road from Jerusalem to Illycricum and beyond. He will lead them home. You can only build the road. So the roads multiply behind you as you faithfully *'be and do'* in the ways of the Serving King. And yes, every homeward-bound traveler delights in the road you have provided as He leads them home. Chase on, there are still road to build...

Day 169

Rumor Evangelism...

"Your purpose is to make your audience see what you saw, hear what you heard, feel what you felt. Relevant detail, couched in concrete, colorful language, is the best way to recreate the incident as it happened and to picture it for the audience." —Dale Carnegie

...and thus I make it my ambition to preach the gospel, not where Christ has already been named, lest I build on someone else's foundation, but as it is written, "Those who have never been told of Him will see, and those who have never heard will understand."
(Romans 15:20-21)

Tragically, evangelism, stories about dynamic adventures with Jesus to those who have not heard, are almost always reduced to *rumors*, stories about someones else's trek after the Serving King. And *rumors*, entertaining as they may be, are rarely persuasive, often repeated, and ultimately futile efforts to build on another's foundation, the bane of evangelism in the mind of the Apostle Paul. Evangelism was never meant to be an endless repetition of entertaining *rumors*, repeating stories of other's encounters with the Serving King. There is a much better way...

Thus, evangelism by *rumor* has no place in the trek after the Serving King. There is a superior way, *evangelism by experience,* the authentic tales of a personal adventures on the heels of the Serving King. These are the stories of actual encounters with the Serving King, first-hand stories of the adventures unfolding in a personal trek. But only those who actually trek after Him have stories to tell, "...couched in concrete, colorful language," stories recent, personal and true, adventures with the Serving King.

And so the tragic death of evangelism, a silent vacuum from those lacking authentic adventures with the Serving King. Lacking personal adventures, transforming encounters with the Serving King, the many return to *rumor evangelism,* stories from the encounters of others, glorious and true, but *rumors* nonetheless. Thus, the many gather week after week to repeat the glorious rumors of old.

But it is never too late to rise from the gathering of the many, to find the path of the Serving King, to begin today's adventure. And be warned, once the adventure begins, you too will refuse to build on another's foundation. Then you will have your own tales of conquest with the Serving King. And yes, "...those who have never heard will understand." Everyone loves a grand tale of adventure in the chase after the Serving King...

Day 170

EXTRA MILE...

"It's never crowded along the extra mile." —Wayne Dyer

This is the reason why I have so often been hindered from coming to you.
But now, since I no longer have any room for work in these regions,
and since I have longed for many years to come to you...
(Romans 15:22-23)

The trek after the Serving King always has an *extra mile*, lonely roads rarely tread upon, meandering miles away from the comfort of the many robustly worshipping the King. Still, the *extra mile* has a well-worn path tread by One looking for those who long ago left the crowd to journey to parts unknown, miles from the safety of the pen, the protection of the crowd. Thus, He rarely joins the crowd, warm and inviting as it may be, ringing with anthems of His praise; instead; He journeys on toward places less crowded, void of the knowledge of Him.

And the few, determined to remain on the heels of the Pathfinder, soon discover there "...is no longer room for work in these regions." Off they must go to places untouched, domains less crowded, the *extra mile*. The *extra mile* is the domain of the Serving King, reserved for those who "...no longer have any room for work in these regions."

The *extra mile* only applies to those whose work in this region is completed, finished, no longer required. And, in that moment, you will be tempted to say, "I am done." Or, perhaps, even the hideous phrase of Kingdom work, "*I am retired.*"

But there is always an *extra mile* in the Kingdom of God. The trek after the Serving King knows no moment of completion, no finish line, no retirement. Instead, there is always an *extra mile,* the lonely road, void of the crowd, the Serving King just ahead. But the *extra mile* is a moment of serendipity, an opportunity to go to those places "...I have longed for many years to come." Here is the freedom to pursue the *secrets of the heart*, the untouched yearnings, the places only dreamed about. Resist the temptation to simply rest in your moment of completion in these regions. Dare to dream. Go the *extra mile as you chase on...*

Day 171

ENJOY THE COMPANY...

"When we love anyone with our whole hearts, life begins when we are with that person; it is only in their company that we are really and truly alive."
—William Barclay

I hope to see you in passing as I go to Spain, and to be helped on my journey there by you, once I have enjoyed your company for a while. At present, however, I am going to Jerusalem bringing aid to the saints.
(Romans 15:24-25)

F ew novices ever really come to understand the exhaustion awaiting those who remain faithfully on the heels of the Serving King. Instead, the many, too enticed by the warmth and comfort of the *company of saints*, settle in for a long visit, a very long visit, basking in the praise and worship of the Serving King. The fellowship of God's people is a seductive elixir, a powerful sedative, an irresistible tonic, for exhausted trekkers on the trail of the Serving King. And you will need to *enjoy the company* from time to time. But those called to the trek after the Serving King must enter carefully, cautiously, leery of the seducing power of the company of those worshipping the Serving King. Few are those able to fight off the urge to stay, to perpetually bask in the praise of God's people, feeding and strengthening the life-giving body, the community of faith.

Understand, the Serving King is almost always on the move, searching for the lost, ever consumed with finding those yet missing at the banquet of praise and worship. He rarely pauses to enjoy the company of the many, cozied up in halls of worship, celebrating life in the bastion of the community of faith. He will visit on occasion, but the halls of worship and praise never hold Him. His is a mission to search out the lost.

The company of saints chasing after the Serving was never intended to be a dwelling place, the persistent gathering of the redeemed, safely housed and protected in mortar and brick. No, this company of saints are nomads, ever intent to remain on the heels of the Serving King, joining Him in His mission to *seek the lost*. Only in His presence, this ever-moving Serving King, are the saints *truly alive*. These are the ones who proclaim, "...once I have enjoyed your company for a while, I am going..." Time to chase on...

Day 172

SHARE...

"By giving people the power to share, we're making the world more transparent." —Mark Zuckerburg

For Macedonia and Achaia have been pleased to make some contribution for the poor among the saints at Jerusalem. For they were pleased to do it, and indeed they owe it to them. For if the Gentiles have come to share in their spiritual blessings, they ought also to be of service to them in material blessings.
(Romans 15:26-27)

The ability to *share*, a grand development in the human condition, rarely comes easily to beings whose first words often express the heartfelt condition of the *inner being*, "No!" and "Mine!" So the vocabulary of most children centers around an acute sense of self-preservation or the more profane, "Looking out for number one." *Sharing* rarely simply appears. It is an acquired way of *'being and doing'*, a learned art form, appearing only in the later stages of human development.

But soon after the quest after the Serving King begins, the call to *share* echoes through the canyons, beckoning all daring to follow Him, to prepare for HIs way of *'being and doing'*, the art of *sharing*, disengaging from those things hindering the quest after the Serving King. The novice, loaded down, unschooled in the difficulties of chasing after the Serving King, too often ignores the echo, shaking off the challenge to disentangle, to *share*. The terrain ahead challenges even the lightest load and cripples the heavy loaded, those slow to disengage from stuff.

Stuff insidiously embeds itself in the very being of those attempting to trek over the steepest grades, long tentacles tenaciously woven around each and every lose fiber of being. Exhausted novices have little chance of *sharing*, ridding themselves of the stuff so easily entangling. But the novice is never alone in their exhaustion and despair. However, the Spirit of the Serving King comes to empower the exhausted, to sever the tentacles of stuff, to enable the novice to lighten the load, to *share*, and move forward under the lighter load.

So they become *pleased to make some contribution to the poor*, liberated from *stuff*, fleet of foot, freed from the burdensome weight of stuff. No, the terrain has not lessened, sloped downhill, nor even flattened out. The novice has simply *shared* as they chase on...

Day 173

FINISHERS...

"The truth is, anyone can start projects. The world is full of just-started projects that looked great at the time but were never completed."
—Joyce Meyer

When therefore I have completed this and have delivered to them what has been collected, I will leave for Spain by way of you. I know that when I come to you I will come in the fullness of the blessing of Christ.
(Romans 15:28-29)

The world is littered with wonderful unfinished enterprises stranded in the realm of *just-started projects* abandoned to pursue another worthy task in the trek after the Serving King. And yes, the trail after the Serving King manifests many worthy distractions in a never-ending stream of opportunities intended for others on the trek after the Serving King. Tragically, the many, too green and inexperienced to complete their own project, flitter from opportunity to opportunity, inhibiting those intended for the task to ever find their rightful place in the calling of the Serving King. Therefore, those flittering from here to there litter the landscape with *just-started projects.*

Completing projects requires much more than the emotional enthusiasm launching far too many projects in the Kingdom God. Enthusiasm wanes in the grueling grind of a myriad of details necessary to bring any *just-started* project to its culminating moment. And most projects require time and energy over the course of many days spent chasing after the Serving King. Such is the nature of relationally-based projects, His ways of *'being and doing'*. Few are those *projects* in the Kingdom requiring less than a great deal of effort.

But the *blessing of Christ* flows toward those who first complete their project before moving toward another. Yet, *finishers* are a rarity in the trek after the Serving King. They, like the Serving King Himself, have learned obedience in the completion of the task assigned, regardless of its cost or the time needed to complete it. *Finishers* never move on until the assignment has been completed. Once concluded, the *blessing of Christ* flows as *finishers* move on toward their next assignment. These are those who getter done in the Kingdom of God. Resist the temptation to litter the landscape with yet another *unfinished enterprise* in the Kingdom of God. Chase on...

Day 174

WEAPONS OF THE WISE...

"Circumstances are rulers of the weak, but they are weapons of the wise"
—Andy Andrews

I appeal to you, brothers, by our Lord Jesus Christ and by the love of the Spirit,
to strive together with me in your prayers to God on my behalf,
that I may be delivered from the unbelievers in Judea, and that
my service for Jerusalem may be acceptable to the saints.
(Romans 15:30-31)

Novices rarely comprehend the *weapons of the wise*; instead, schooled in old ways of *'being and doing'*, novices continue fighting in the old ways, winning skirmishes of all kinds, yet losing the war. The temptation to fight with old and familiar tools is often too much for the novice to ignore, and so the *weapons of the wise* remain dormant, unused, and untapped resources from the Serving King.

Paul is no novice, hence, his decision to call for the *weapons of the wise* as the saints *strive together*. He has discovered circumstances do no more than challenge the *wise* to engage with *weapons* of another kind, the *weapons of the wise*, His ways of *'being and doing'*. So the challenge to *pray*, to unleash the power of God in circumstances dire.

But prayer, the *weapon of the wise*, is exhausting, the most challenging of all weapons of war. Few are able to wield this *weapon of the wise*. It mandates utter reliance upon God, a refusal to fight in the ways of old, a reckless abandonment to His ways of *'being and doing'.* Prayer is no surrendering to mere circumstances; rather, it is confidence in God to bring about profound changes in circumstances through the power of prayer "...that I may be delivered."

You will be tempted in the early days of the trek after the Serving King to fight with the old ways, but it is not His way. He is not content with simple victory, but victory the result of the *weapon of the wise*. Resist the urge to engage with the old ways. You cannot please the Serving King winning battles with the old weapons. There is but one way to engage with the *weapon of the wise*: Pray. It is the power for those who chase on...

Day 175

REFRESHED...

*"In the sweetness of friendship let there be laughter, and sharing of pleasures.
For in the dew of little things the heart finds its morning and is refreshed."*
—Khalil Gibran

*...so that by God's will I may come to you with joy and be refreshed in your
company. May the God of peace be with you all. Amen.*
(Romans 15:32-33)

Fatigue often appears in those chasing after the Serving King, worn-out road builders, the inevitable by-product of a life poured into the quest. The novice, ignorant of the impending fatigue, often ignores the necessity of a consistent refreshing as the saints gather. So the gathering of the saints goes unattended, day after day, week after week, month after month, as fatigue relentlessly pursues those on the trek after the Serving King. And fatigue is a serious foe, mandating an equally serious response equipping those deepest into of the trek to carry on in spite of the impending fatigue.

You are ill-suited to pursue the Serving King in isolation, away from the refreshing of the saints. Those succeeding in the quest learn the necessity of isolation with the King, reinforced by the refreshing of the company of saints. In the gathering of the saints, stories of unexpected adventure are exchanged, wounds healed, the balm of encouragement liberally applied with challenges to carry on, sustenance for the journey freely given.

So the necessity of well-planned gatherings of the saints. Hinderances of all kinds will appear, temptations to gather elsewhere, but you must resist. Your presence is needed. You are not only a recipient, you are also a giver of nourishment for the exhausted chasers who gather. This is a mutual edification gathering, the body of Christ at its best.

But life is hectic, more hectic than you imagined, so comes the temptation to skip the gathering, to remain in the rat race, running on the wheel that never stops. Or, perhaps, a nap, sleep for the weary. So they gather without you, celebrating lives well lived, comforting those in need of the balm of fellowship. But they will not gather long. Refreshed, the chasers carry on with or without you. Join the celebration, the rat race will wait for you, it always does. Chase on...

Day 176

WELCOME MATS...

"People will always be tempted to wipe their feet on anything with 'welcome' written on it." —Andy Partridge

I commend to you our sister Phoebe, a servant of the church at Cenchreae, that you may welcome her in the Lord in a way worthy of the saints, and help her in whatever she may need from you, for she has been a patron of many and of myself as well.
(Romans 16:1-2)

Welcome mats often tell the tale of those gathering behind the door. Some mats, bright and shiny, never see the soles of travelers, never greet those whose journeys have managed to find this isolated spot. This mat is rarely used by those fortunate enough to find the trail to this door. Few are those who leave this room to rub shoulders with those on trails unknown. So they gather week after week, safe and secure, in a room found by few.

Other mats, worn and often used, welcome countless sojourners at the end of a well-worn trail. This mat proclaims the door is open to all comers, anyone finding their way to this room, any sojourner in need of comfort and encouragement. This mat sees the feet of many who come to their room.

Sojourners, those most serious about the chase after the Serving King, are never content to simply meet with those well-known, those whose paths often cross. No, these sojourners often leave the comfort of the room, looking for those who as yet have not found their way to the room at the end of the trail. These sojourners know the loneliness and exhaustion of journeys long and arduous. So they share hospitality with those they encounter along the way, "... for she has been a patron of many and of myself as well." They, too, strangers to the room behind the welcome mat, need a time to gather with the saints, those whose journeys cycle to the same place, with the same folks, week after week. So Paul's exhortation to welcome those whose journeys bring them to your door.

Examine the *welcome mat* at the door of the room where you often gather. Is the mat worn and dusty, filled with the soil of exhausted sojourners longing for the comfort of the room behind the mat? No chase after the Serving King is meant to be spent in the room behind the mat. Chase on until you to have found that sojourner who longs to wipe their feet at the *welcome mat* at your door...

Day 177

RISKED NECKS...

"A ship is safe in harbor, but that's not what ships are for."
—William G. T. Shed

Greet Prisca and Aquila, my fellow workers in Christ Jesus,
who risked their necks for my life, to whom not only I give thanks but
all the churches of the Gentiles give thanks as well.
(Romans 16:3-4)

For those deepest in the quest after the Serving King, *safe harbor* no longer appeals, no more tempts the seaworthy ship and crew to remain in calm waters, avoiding the very purpose for which they were created. Instead, *fellow workers*, those chasing deepest after the Serving King, have embraced a new way of *'being and doing'*, risky in every way, rough seas the expected way of life, no sea too rough to encumber the quest after the Serving King. Today, however, marks the return of one *fellow worker*, one whose *risked neck* survived for another day, another adventure on the heels of the Serving King.

But not all trekkers make it beyond safe harbor. Unable or too intimidated, some remain in quiet waters awaiting the return of those who have risked much for the sake of the Kingdom of God. But they, too, those who remain in calm waters, have a significant place in the Kingdom of God, a role designed by the King for those unable to man the decks of ships soon seaward bound for the roughest seas.

These are the *greeters*, those who pamper both returning ship and sailor. They are the encouragers, the financiers, the suppliers, the cheerleaders, those who recognize the value of the *risked necks* coming closest to the cross awaiting us all. So the *greeters* soothe the aching necks of those who have risked much for the Kingdom of God.

And there will be days when joining the sailors on the roughest seas lures you to abandon your role, to leave behind the *greeter's* task, to man the decks of seaworthy ships. But not every neck is meant to be risked. So resist the temptation to leap onto the deck of the seaward bound. Wait for His call, His mandate to join the crew, and, in the meantime, *greet my fellow workers* as they chase on...

Day 178

SILENCE...

"Referring to the church as a building is like referring to people as two-by-fours." —Don Everts

Greet also the church in their house. Greet my beloved Epaenetus, who was the first convert to Christ in Asia. Greet Mary, who has worked hard for you.
(Romans 16:5–6)

Moderns, long accustomed to church as brick and mortar, often misunderstand the challenge to *"...greet the Church in their house."* And so, the deafening modern *silence* of God's people enter shrines of brick and mortar dedicated to silence. Silence is the way of brick and mortar, tongueless, unable to *greet* or proclaim the goodness of God, to embrace the warmth of fellowship. Silence is the language of stones. But silence is not His way of *'being and doing'*.

People, the brick and mortar of the church, are not well-suited for silence. Silence is rarely their way *'being and doing'*. People, unaccustomed to the deafening silence of brick and mortar, too often avoid the places of silence engaged in quiet worship of the Serving King. Silence is foreign for those accustomed to *greeting*. Silence makes no accommodation for the unruliness of people too excited to gather in *silence*. So they gather in places where *greeting* is welcomed and encouraged, and the stones bask in the silence, the language of brick and mortar.

But brick and mortar provide safety and comfort for the noisy gathering of God's people, the Church, enthusiastically engaging in the art of *greeting*, the robust gathering of the church. And speak they must, energized from adventures on the heels of the Serving King. So begins the *greeting* of God's people as they gather in houses of worship, shrines of brick and mortar designed for *greeting*, His way of *'being and doing'*.

There will be no *silence* as the people of God gather. They are the *greeters*, the noisy community, the storytellers, the proclaimers of Good News, the band of brothers, united in tales of adventure with the Serving King. And so His proclamation, "I tell you, if these were silent, the very stones would cry out." The chase is never silent...

Day 179

UNORDINARY PRISONERS...

"I'm not an ordinary prisoner." —*Mikhail Khodorkovsky*

Greet Andronicus and Junia, my kinsmen and my fellow prisoners.
They are well known to the apostles, and they were in Christ before me.
Greet Ampliatus, my beloved in the Lord.
(Romans 16:7-8)

P aul, deeply immeshed in the trek after the Serving King, often describes himself as a prisoner *for* the Lord and *of* the Lord. Understandable for a man captured by the Serving King on the Damascus Road. But he was not the first of many captured by the persuasive power and presence of the Serving King. And make no underestimation, he was indeed captured in every sense of the word. But he merely joins the ranks of the privileged few genuinely captured by the Serving King. Those deepest in the trek after the Serving King may soon discover they too have been captured not only by the persuasive passion of the Serving King, but, likewise, by His opponents engaging in every foreseeable distraction and power to hinder the work of the prisoners of the Lord.

But these are no ordinary prisoners; rather, they are the unordinary prisoners of the Serving King named by the King and unleashed into His service. There is no power, no hindrance, no force, capable of preventing the unordinary prisoner of the Lord from accomplishing the task He has fashioned for His beloved. And they are His beloved, claimed by the King, adopted as children, never abandoned, never ordinary prisoners. Thus, His beloved proclaim, "I'm not an ordinary prisoner, nor am I alone. I am an unordinary prisoner of the Serving King."

This is the great mystery of all unordinary prisoners. They are never alone, always in Christ, ever on task, relentlessly pursuing the call of the Serving King. It is in their captivity, both in Him and for Him, that they shine forth as beacons for a lost and dying world of ordinary prisoners. In the end, we are all prisoners of one kind or another, either to sin or the Serving King. The only question remaining is the kind of prisoner you will be. Will you be amongst the many, mere ordinary prisoners, or will you join the ranks of the unordinary prisoners captured by the Serving King? Time to join the chase of the unordinary...

Day 180

APPROVED IN CHRIST...

"Nothing is as approved as mediocrity, the majority has established it and it fixes it fangs on whatever gets beyond it either way."
—Blaise Pascal

Greet Urbanus, our fellow worker in Christ, and my beloved Stachys.
Greet Apelles, who is approved in Christ. Greet those who
belong to the family of Aristobulus.
(Romans 16:9-10)

Few chasing after the Serving King rise above mediocrity, a run-of-the-mill approach to Christlikeness, a middle-of-the-road status, the comfort of hanging with those content with plain, old normal. So the many run together, a gathering of the like-minded, each resembling every other. But, occasionally an Apelles appears, quietly receiving the highest of praise, the label often missed by the casual reader, reserved only for him, a one-of-kind, a truly unique follower of the Serving King. Only Apelles receives the glorious label, *"...approved in Christ."*

Nowhere else does Paul bestow such accolades for those deepest in the trek after the Serving King, only here and only to Apelles. The term simply means to examine a thing carefully, to demonstrate its essence, its quality, and its true nature. Only he rises to such status, quietly and unobtrusively, buried in the long list of greetings from the Apostle Paul.

The community of faith knows relatively nothing about him. Few ever hear his name, even know he existed, approved quietly in the community of faith, one single line bearing his name. But, oh, the significance of this one *approved in Christ.* Such is the life of those deepest into the quest after the Serving King. They quietly mimic the Serving King, serving in the mundane things, unobserved and invaluable to the body of Christ.

They have succeeded in resisting the mandate to be normal, to remain in the pack, to avoid the *fangs of the majority.* They are persistent in seeking the approval of only the Serving King, the Christ. Only He carries any significance for these modern *Apelles.* Look closely and you will see them, *approved in Christ,* quietly and efficiently *'being and doing'* in the ways of the Serving King. Chase on...

Day 181

WORKED HARD...

"We need people who can actually do things. We have too many bosses and too few workers." —Andy Rooney

Greet my kinsman Herodion. Greet those in the Lord who belong to the family of Narcissus. Greet those workers in the Lord, Tryphaena and Tryphosa. Greet the beloved Persis, who has worked hard in the Lord.
(Romans 16:11-12)

Novices rarely understand the trek after the Serving King is more work than they have ever known. But it is not the work of drudgery; rather, it's the glorious work of the Kingdom, serving in His way of *'being and doing'*, unleashed into the mundane of everyday living. Misunderstanding the concept of work, the novice too often avoids all work, fearful it will merely be more of what life has offered already, meaningless, repetitive drudgery of all kinds, exhausting both body and soul. But such is not the way of the Serving King.

His yoke is easy (Matthew 11:30) and He offers it to all those willing to work in the Kingdom of God. Work is the reckless, passionate pursuit of His way of *'being and doing'* in the minutiae of life, bringing life to the mundane. Hence, there is no meaningless drudgery in the Kingdom of God, rather, the powerful transformation of the mundane into the meaningful and significant. So He leads His kinsman into life-giving activities for both the worker and the recipient of work.

Nonetheless, the novice, damaged by the drudgery of the mundane, hesitates at the trailhead, fearful to engage in the work of the Serving King. Having no experience with a boss of this kind, the novice rarely steps in to the privilege of working for the Serving King, thereby, surrendering the life-giving energy of *'being and doing'* in the ways of the Serving King.

But there are those pursuers understanding the privilege and rewards of working hard for the Serving King, recklessly engaging in any work the Serving King makes available. They have learned the rewards of the hard work made available by the Serving King. Theirs is a life of joy and passion. And no greater reward for these hard workers than hearing the proclamation of the Serving King, "Well done, good and faithful servant." Chase on...

Day 182

UNCHOSEN…

"You have been chosen, and you must therefore use such strength and heart and wits as you have." —J. R. R. Tolken

Greet Rufus, chosen in the Lord; also his mother, who has been a mother to me as well. Greet Asyncritus, Phlegon, Hermes, Patrobas, Hermas, and the brothers who are with them.
(Romans 16:13-14)

Every child knows the glorious joy of being *chosen* and the horrible agony of being left out, an afterthought, waiting on the sidelines for a moment in the sun. Moments of *chosen* are glorious, filled with sensations of inclusion, bathed in the warmth of being desired, called out from the many to join the ranks of the *chosen,* the wanted, the valued, the elite. No greater joy than being known, *chosen*, included, named, as a valued member of the community of faith.

But the Serving King is never content to see familiar names in letters from the saints, to gather with familiar *chosen* ones, to bask in the fellowship of the *chosen*. His is a mission for the lost, the yet *unchosen*, the unnamed faces in the masses. And there can be no rest for Him until every *unchosen* comes face-to-face with Him, provided opportunity to be amongst the *chosen*.

So the *chosen* soon discover a responsibility toward the others, the *unchosen*, names called later or not at all, faces lost in the crowd of the many. Hence, the need to "…use such strength and heart and wits as you have," such is the responsibility of the *chosen* in the trek after the Serving King. They have been *chosen* for a reason, an invitation to join Him in a quest to find the *unchosen*, those still secretly longing to know the joy of being *chosen,* recognized by the Serving King.

And so, the dream of every *unchosen* is to be amongst the selected, the named. It is the crowning moment of every life to see your name in the letter that really matters, the *Book of Life*. So the Serving King proclaims, *"…I will never blot out his name from the book of life"* (Revelation 3:5). Chase on until you are in the book…

Day 183

ALL THE SAINTS...

*"I am not a saint, unless you think of a saint as a sinner
who keeps on trying." —Nelson Mandela*

*Greet Philologus, Julia, Nereus and his sister, and Olympas,
and all the saints who are with them. Greet one another with a holy kiss.
All the churches of Christ greet you.
(Romans 16:15-16)*

The community of faith has damaged the term, unintentionally rendering it almost useless, providing no favors to those hoping to use the term to describe people chasing after the Serving King. Saint, too often, refers to the end of the journey, the highest stage of transformation in the life of those deepest in the trek, a lofty goal available only to the rarest few, the best-of-the-best. But saint merely identifies those on the trek, regardless of location on the quest or even the particular stage of transformation manifesting in the life of one following the Serving King

But, it is not too late to reclaim the term, to redefine it, and again deploy it as Paul intended, the moniker of those chasing after the Serving King. Saint is meant to reflect a condition of the heart, a way of 'being and doing', the effort to trek after the Serving King. It never points to the externals themselves, rather, to the transformation of *being* occurring within those chasing after the Serving King.

Still, there is good reason for the confusion. The trek after the Serving King is always, yes always, effective in bringing about visible transformation in those persistent in the quest, hence, the confusion. The saint, ever persistent in pursuing the Serving King, cannot escape the transformation of life, of *being* and consequent *doing*, accompanying the trek. Transformation of externals, visible to all in proximity, cannot be stripped away from those earnestly pursuing the trail of the King. Novices, unable to discern the transformation of the heart, of *being*, mistakenly label externals as evidence pointing to the presence of a *saint*.

You will be hesitant to use the label, to allow others to call you saint. You have determined it appropriate only for those farther down the trail. But, be of good cheer, the externals will catch up soon enough. And you, too, will rest comfortably in the label saint. Chase on as a saint...

Day 184

ILLUSIONS...

*"The greatest obstacle to discovery is not ignorance -
it is the illusion of knowledge." —Daniel J. Boorstin*

*I appeal to you, brothers, to watch out for those who cause divisions and
create obstacles contrary to the doctrine that you have been taught; avoid
them. For such persons do not serve our Lord Christ, but their own appetites,
and by smooth talk and flattery they deceive the hearts of the naive.
(Romans 16:17)*

Wisdom, the late arriver in the trek after the Servant King, often eludes the confident novice in the early days of the quest, basking in the warmth of superficial knowledge, certain the trail ahead is the right one. But, eventually, every trekker discovers the trail is not so simple as originally thought, soon littered with lost souls, confused by the myriad of voices pointing this way toward trails of every kind. Learning to hear His voice above all other voices comes too late for many on the quest.

Bewildered by the cacophony of voices, the novice often abandons the quest, confused to carry on, crippled by uncertainty. Or they follow this or that voice, joining one clan or another, comforted by the illusion of knowledge, the ease of the trail and the warmth of the crowd. Many, confident in the illusion, never find again the heels of the Serving King, content to live in the comfort of the illusion shared by the many.

But there are those who refuse to live in the company of the illusion, smooth talk and flattery comforting the soul of the naïve. They are the company of the few avoiding those who distract with illusions of flattery, determined to remain on the heels of the Serving King. They cannot be distracted, nor dissuaded, ignoring signs pointing to easier trails built for ease and comfort.

Wisdom comes from the mouth of the Serving King. And those who learn to hear His voice never lose their way. Many will attempt to distract them, raised voices threatening to drown out the voice of the King. But those deepest in the quest learn to avoid the noisemakers, instead remaining on the heels of the Serving King, close enough to always hear His voice above all other voices. Such is the way of Wisdom in the chase after the Serving King...

Day 185

APPETITES...

"A well governed appetite is the greater part of liberty."
—Lucius Annaeus Seneca

*For such persons do not serve our Lord Christ, but their own appetites,
and by smooth talk and flattery they deceive the hearts of the naive.
(Romans 16:18)*

Herod, skilled in the art of *smooth talk,* mistook the *magi,* wisemen from the East, as naive fools, void of a relationship with Him who leads the *wise* into life's greatest discoveries. But he was greatly mistaken. The wisemen, the Magi, easily recognized through the power of the Holy Spirit, he who was merely seeking a way to feed his own appetite, a lust for power. So the Magi do not return to Herod, recognizing the voracious appetite of a king determined to remain in power.

But Herod is not alone in his quest to feed his appetite on Christmas Day. Christmas has become the ultimate appetite day, feedings of all kinds rage throughout the day, hindering those on the quest to find the newborn King. The King, quietly hidden deep off the beaten trail, tucked away in the safety of the manger, continues to wait patiently for those persistent in finding their way to Him, those whose appetites are held at bay until the true King has been found. They have no time for eating. Only when the King has been found will modern magi find time to eat.

Instead, modern magi continue the search, asking any and every Herod, those who should know His whereabouts, where He can be found. But few are those who have managed to *govern* their appetite, maintaining Jesus the center of Christmas, keeping at bay any appetite threatening to consume the quest for the Serving King. So the modern Herods send the magi here and there proclaiming interest in the newborn King while they feast until the King has been found. But modern magi, like the magi of old, know the self-serving Herods of today.

Watch Herod eat, and you too will see the appetite revealing the heart. Only those who have governed the appetite will abandon the feast. Off they go. The chase on continues in earnest...

Day 186

THE BETTER SERMON...

"One act of obedience is better than one hundred sermons."
—*Dietrich Bonhoeffer*

For your obedience is known to all, so that I rejoice over you, but I want you to be wise as to what is good and innocent as to what is evil.
(Romans 16:19)

Many are those who love to talk, especially, in modern communities of faith. Gatherings of all kinds are filled with *talking heads*, people who love to discuss what obedience would look like for those chasing after the Serving King. Even pastors are easily subdued, enthralled with words, talkers of the best kind. So churches fill with those radically committed to talking. Alas, talking has become an end in itself. And, tragically, talking does little to increase the reputation of those chasing after the Serving King.

But there is a better way, the way of obedience. It is obedience which catches the ear of those exhausted by the endless barrage of words coming from those who love to talk. Obedience, noise the ear cannot ignore, builds the reputation of those chasing after the Serving King. It is the fruit of *'being'* which manifests itself in the activity of doing. And *'being'* is rarely enhanced by talking. Instead, *'being'* is enriched simply by dwelling in the presence of the Serving King. It is those who learn to first dwell in His presence, who then learn to *'do'*, to engage in His way of *'being and doing'*. Obedience rises up out of authentic encounters with the Serving King.

Be warned, obedience leaves little time for mere talking. Instead, days will be filled with the activity of obedience. Day-after-day obedience fills the hours with seamless activity for the Serving King.

And then arrives the unexpected fruit: something new to talk about. No need to repeat the stories of old, to theorize about what Jesus might like to be done. In place of the old tales are brand new ones, adventures of the present moment, stories about what He is doing not did. Your stories will fill the air. Unexpectedly, a crowd begins to build as "...your obedience is known to all." And they, too, will "...rejoice over you." These are the best of stories as you chase after the Serving King...

Day 187

CRUSHED...

"He who puts out his hand to stop the wheel of
history will have his fingers crushed." —Lech Walesa

The God of peace will soon crush Satan under your feet.
The grace of our Lord Jesus Christ be with you.
(Romans 16:20)

Only the fool, the most arrogant of the arrogant, would dare to grab the wheel of God's history. Nonetheless, he grabs it over and over again, each time crushed by the feet of those who have learned to go for the ride as God's wheel ushers in His-story. Still, the old fool, perhaps groggy from the feet of some many across the millenniums, continues to grab the wheel of those chasing after the Serving King, hopeful to derail just a few. But his is a mission of folly, unable to deter those chasing after the Serving King.

No surprise, for long ago, the King announced the futility of the fool and the promise of the feet of Him who would crush Satan under His feet, "I will put enmity between you and the woman, and between your offspring and her offspring; He shall bruise your head" (Genesis 3:15). Thinking such words mere boasting, confident in his own ability, the lummox continues on the errand of a fool. But fall from heaven he will, ousted by the Serving King.

Satan, bruised yet undeterred, thinking only the Serving King can crush, foolishly still engages, suffering the ongoing bruising of those whose feet continue to crush the fool. Like Wiley Coyote, he continues to believe that one day the 'roadrunner' will be caught, finally a meal when the day draws to a close. But it is not really the chaser whose foot crushes the persistent nemesis. No, it is the King Himself who continues to crush Satan under the feet of those chasing after the Serving King.

Like Dorothy, shocked at killing the Wicked Witch, you will also proclaim, "I didn't mean to kill her, really I didn't. It's just..." Rest assured, it is not you who crushes Satan under your foot. It was He who continually places Satan under the feet of His children as they simply chase on...

Day 188

THE WRITER AND TRUE FRIEND...

*"It is not often that someone comes along who is a true friend
and a good writer." —E. B. White*

*Timothy, my fellow worker, greets you; so do Lucius and Jason and Sosipater,
my kinsmen. I Tertius, who wrote this letter, greet you in the Lord.
(Romans 16:21-22)*

Some stories simply have to be told, even if the tale is not your story. So Tertius spent countless hours writing stories that were not his own, tales from the lips of another, wisdom for the generations yet to come. He was captured by Him, spent his life telling the stories of those who championed the cause of the chase after the Serving King. History rarely mentions his name, countless are those blessed by the witness of that rare writer who was also a good friend. Paul was surrounded by the rarest of finds, *the writer and good friend.*

Paul, famous beyond description, was blessed with good friends, men and women who cherished their relationship with him. Together, they all, each of them, accomplished much for the Kingdom of God. Each played a critical role within the Kingdom, accomplishing more as a melded unit than any of them would have accomplished in isolation. Working in tandem, they produced the letters that would change the world.

You will be tempted to think only their stories are worthy of the telling, worthy of writing, powerful enough to change the lives of many. But understand, the power of the oldest story is not what it accomplished in the past, but what it is bringing about in the present moment. So every new story is added to the oldest of stories, each proclaiming the power of *story* in days gone by and days yet to come.

Resist the temptation to tell no stories. Everyone has a story, tales of the chase after the Serving King, adventures in the mundane, stories of how the Serving King transformed the lives of those in the chase. How you tell the story matters not. Whether by pen or pencil, camera or phone, Facebook or Instagram, everyone has a story. Tell the stories of how the Serving King stepped into the mundane of your life and added to the greatest tale of all. Add your chapter to the story as you chase on after the Serving King...

Day 189

NO STRANGERS...

"Smile at a stranger and see what happens."
—*Patti Lupone*

Gaius, who is host to me and to the whole church, greets you. Erastus, the city treasurer, and our brother Quartus, greet you.
(Romans 16:23)

The chase after the Serving King often makes *strangers* of us all. Rarely does the Serving King allow you to remain in lands well-known, familiar people at every turn, trails clearly marked. It simply is not His way. Instead, those chasing after the Serving King often find themselves *strangers* in a new land. So comes the importance of learning the role of *host* for all those whose chase leads them into your domain.

The land is filled with *strangers*, people living side by side, too busy for the messiness of authentic greetings, hellos filled with meaning and purpose, relationships initiated. So the passing quips of those too engaged in moving along to genuinely *greet* those *strangers* now in their midst.

But those long engaged in the chase after the Serving King know the importance, more than that, the power, of a greeting well done. It is the seasoned chasers, those who have traveled long and hard, who greet those newest in the land. It is they who offer the hand of fellowship, the warmth of a smile, the invitation to break bread together.

And then it happens, almost instantaneously, effortlessly, the power of the Kingdom at work, the *'stranger'* disappears. In the *stranger's* place, a new brother, a new sister, a new companion for this chase after the Serving King. There are no strangers in the Kingdom of God. It simply cannot be where those chasing after the Serving King gather. They know and live with the fellowship of the people of God, brothers and sisters united by the power of the Spirit. Theirs is a family of a special kind.

So the challenge to *'greet'* any would-be strangers in your midst. Risk a new adventure into relationships yet unknown. Such is the way of the Kingdom, the way of those who have traveled long and far in the chase after the Serving King...

Day 190

NEVER TO LATE...

"It is never too late to strengthen the foundation of faith. There is always time. With faith in the Savior, you can repent and plead for forgiveness. There is someone you can forgive. There is someone you can thank. There is someone you can serve and lift. You can do it wherever you are and however alone and deserted you may feel." —Henry B. Eyring

Now to Him who is able to strengthen you according to my gospel and the preaching of Jesus Christ, according to the revelation of the mystery that was kept secret for long ages but has now been disclosed and through the prophetic writings has been made known to all nations, according to the command of the eternal God, to bring about the obedience of faith—.
(Romans 16:25-26)

Those traveling deepest into the quest after the Serving King know the energy needed to finish the trek, to remain on the heels of Him who leads to the highest mountains. They have discovered the secret kept hidden for so many years from so many people, now known to anyone who dares to ask. They have discovered the Serving King worthy of following. They have also discovered this is no easy trek.

But this Serving King waits for no man, charging onward, accomplishing all that God the Father has called Him to accomplish. Those daring to stay the trek soon discover the strength needed to remain on His heels is far beyond the abilities of any mere human. To sustain the trek requires a strengthening from on high from God who strengthens even the Serving King. Without it, no one can sustain the trek into the highest realms.

Here, so close to the end of the quest, the fatigue can be overwhelming. So the final climbs require the greatest energy of all, these final steps into the last stages of Christlikeness: Christian maturity reflecting His way of *'being and doing'*. Those still in the chase late in the day have learned the secret to the needed stamina in the last days: intimacy with the Serving King.

But some will fear it is too late to make the final climbs, to enter into these last stages of development. Rest assured, it is never too late. God often does His best work in the final days of those chasing after the Serving King, days in which the distractions of life are finally winding down. Simply ask for the strength to climb the hills still to come. These are the best days yet in the chase after the Serving King...

Day 191

THE WISEST...

"I know that I am intelligent, because I know that I know nothing."
—Socrates

...to the only wise God be glory forevermore through Jesus Christ! Amen.
(Romans 16:27)

Confidence brimming, the chase after the Serving King finally begins in earnest. It is only in the latter days of the quest that the chaser finally begins to understand so little is yet known, so far yet to go, even at this late stage of the quest. And yet, the chaser is eager to continue on in the final trails yet ahead. It is they, those who have chased long and hard, who join with Socrates in proclaiming, "...because I know that I know nothing." Only God, filled with wisdom, knows what can be known. And there is so much yet to be known, yet to be experienced, even for the most seasoned chasers.

So the wisest of chasers wind down the quest after the Serving King knowing they are about to finally embrace the final teachings of "...the only wise God." Still, it is only in the final days of the quest that the veteran chaser genuinely understands just how far the chase has taken them. Looking back, the trail of the quest stretches far over the horizon, countless miles and journeys, all leading to this final trail, this final chase, after the Serving King.

It is in that moment, brief as it may be, that those chasing longest and hardest finally understand just how much God has done in their lives, how much things have really changed, how blessed life has really been across the many routes of days gone by. Profoundly aware of all that God has done, the wisest chasers join Paul in proclaiming, "...to the only wise God be glory forevermore through Jesus Christ."

It is the song of the redeemed, those touched and transformed by the grace of God. They have chased long and hard on the heels of the Serving King. Oh, the joy of having come so far. But the chase is not quite over. One final trail to begin. Chase on...

EPILOGUE

L ike the two volume set *Mornings With Oswald* and *More Mornings with Oswald (Xulon Press, 2014)*, *Chasing God* is a two volume set. Volume one ends with the conclusion of Romans chapter 7. Volume 2, *More Chasing God*, *picked up* the conversation with Romans chapter 8.

Don and his wife Laura have also published a book on marriage, *31 Days To Paradise*, available anywhere books are sold.

ABOUT THE AUTHOR

D on is an avid, extreme hiker, exploring trail after trail across the Grand Canyon. But, now long in the tooth, he frequently finds himself 'chasing' the young hikers strolling along miles ahead. And so came the idea of 'chasing after God'.

Don attended Drexel University in downtown Philadelphia before transferring to Northwest Nazarene University in Nampa, Idaho, where he earned a BA in Philosophy and Religion, followed by seminary in Kansas City (Master of Divinity), and concluding with a Dr. of Ministry in 2006. He has pastored in a variety of settings from the heart of downtown Phoenix, to the back roads of a rural farm community in Missouri, to the inner city of Indianapolis, to the coastal beauty of Oregon, and the charming southern culture of South Carolina, and currently serves as the Lead Pastor for the FlagNaz Community Church of the Nazarene in Flagstaff, Arizona.

Pay It Forward

Every now and then, I pull up to the cashiers at Starbucks only to be told, "The car ahead of you paid for your coffee this morning." I always grin and pay for the car behind me (and I dare not look to see how many are in the car!). I have started doing the same thing with the books I enjoy. If I have enjoyed a good book, I buy another copy and pass it along. If you have found this book to be a blessing in your life, we encourage you to pay it forward.

Let Us Hear From You

We always enjoy hearing from those of you who journey along with us.

Feel free to contact me at: revminter@me.com

CPSIA information can be obtained
at www.ICGtesting.com
Printed in the USA
FSHW02n0409151018
53016FS